CAMBRIDGE

CB127940

B2 FIRST 4

WITH ANSWERS

AUTHENTIC PRACTICE TESTS

WITH AUDIO

WITH RESOURCE BANK

Cambridge University Press
www.cambridge.org/elt

Cambridge Assessment English
www.cambridgeenglish.org

Information on this title: www.cambridge.org/9781108780148

© Cambridge University Press and Cambridge Assessment 2020

It is normally necessary for written permission for copying to be obtained *in advance* from a publisher. The sample answer sheets at the back of this book are designed to be copied and distributed in class.
The normal requirements are waived here and it is not necessary to write to Cambridge University Press for permission for an individual teacher to make copies for use within his or her own classroom. Only those pages that carry the wording '© Cambridge Assessment 2020 Photocopiable' may be copied.

First published 2020

20 19 18 17 16 15 14 13 12 11 10 9 8 7 6 5

Printed in Poland by Opolgraf

A catalogue record for this publication is available from the British Library

ISBN 978-1-108-78014-8 B2 First 4 Student's Book with Answers with Audio
ISBN 978-1-108-74810-0 B2 First 4 Student's Book without answers

The publishers have no responsibility for the persistence or accuracy of URLs for external or third-party internet websites referred to in this publication, and do not guarantee that any content on such websites is, or will remain, accurate or appropriate. Information regarding prices, travel timetables, and other factual information given in this work is correct at the time of first printing but the publishers do not guarantee the accuracy of such information thereafter.

Contents

Introduction

Prepare for the exam with practice tests from Cambridge

Inside you'll find four authentic examination papers from Cambridge Assessment English. They are the perfect way to practise – EXACTLY like the real exam.

Why are they unique?

All our authentic practice tests go through the same design process as the *B2 First* exam. We check every single part of our practice tests with real students under exam conditions, to make sure we give you the most authentic experience possible.

Students can practise these tests on their own or with the help of a teacher to familiarise themselves with the exam format, understand the scoring system and practise exam technique.

Cambridge English Qualifications	CEFR Level	UK National Qualifications
C2 Proficiency	C2	3
C1 Advanced	C1	2
B2 First	B2	1
B1 Preliminary	B1	Entry 3
A2 Key	A2	Entry 2

Further information

The information contained in this practice book is designed to be an overview of the exam. For a full description of all of the above exams, including information about task types, testing focus and preparation, please see the relevant handbooks which can be obtained from the Cambridge Assessment English website at: **cambridgeenglish.org.**

The structure of *B2 First:* an overview

The *Cambridge English Qualifications B2 First* examination consists of four papers:

Reading and Use of English: 1 hour 15 minutes
In Parts 1 to 4, the test contains texts with accompanying grammar and vocabulary tasks, and separate items with a grammar and vocabulary focus. In Parts 5 to 7, the test contains a range of texts and accompanying reading comprehension tasks.

Writing: 1 hour 20 minutes
In Part 1, which is **compulsory**, candidates have to write an essay of between 140 and 190 words, giving their opinion in response to a task. In Part 2, there are three tasks from which candidates choose **one** to write about. The range of tasks from which questions may be drawn includes an article, an email or letter, a report and a review. In this part, candidates have to write between 140 and 190 words.

Listening: 40 minutes approximately
Each part contains a recorded text or texts and some questions, including multiple-choice, sentence completion and multiple-matching questions. Each text is heard twice.

Speaking: 14 minutes (or 20 minutes for groups of 3)
The standard test format is two candidates and two examiners. Candidates will be given photographs and other visual and written material to look at and talk about.

	Overall length	Number of tasks/parts	Number of items
Reading and Use of English	1 hour 15 minutes	7	52
Writing	1 hour 20 minutes	2	-
Listening	approx. 40 mins	4	30
Speaking	14–20 mins	4	-
Total	3 hours 30 mins approximately		

Grading

All candidates receive a Statement of Results and candidates whose performance ranges between CEFR Levels B1 and C1 (Cambridge English Scale scores of 140–190) also receive a certificate.

- Candidates who achieve **Grade A** (Cambridge English Scale scores of 180–190) receive the First Certificate in English stating that they demonstrated ability at Level C1.
- Candidates who achieve **Grade B** or **C** (Cambridge English Scale scores of 160–179) receive the First Certificate in English at Level B2.
- Candidates whose performance is below B2 level, but falls within **Level B1** (Cambridge English Scale scores of 140–159), receive a Cambridge English certificate stating that they have demonstrated ability at Level B1.
- For further information on grading and results, go to the website (see page 4 for details).

Speaking: an overview for candidates

You take the Speaking test with another candidate (possibly two candidates), referred to here as your partner. There are two examiners. One will speak to you and your partner and the other will be listening. Both examiners will award marks.

Part 1 (2 minutes)

The examiner asks you and your partner questions about yourselves. You may be asked about things like 'your home town', 'your interests', 'your career plans', etc.

Part 2 (a one-minute 'long turn' for each candidate, plus a 30-second response from the second candidate)

The examiner gives you two photographs and asks you to talk about them for one minute. The examiner then asks your partner a question about your photographs and your partner responds briefly.

Then the examiner gives your partner two different photographs. Your partner talks about these photographs for one minute. This time the examiner asks you a question about your partner's photographs and you respond briefly.

Part 3 (4 minutes)

The examiner asks you and your partner to talk together. They give you a task to look at so you can think about and discuss an idea, giving reasons for your opinion. For example, you may be asked to think about some changes in the world, or about spending free time with your family. After you have discussed the task for about two minutes with your partner, the examiner will ask you a follow-up question, which you should discuss for a further minute.

Part 4 (4 minutes)

The examiner asks some further questions, which leads to a more general discussion of what you have talked about in Part 3. You may comment on your partner's answers if you wish.

Test 1

READING AND USE OF ENGLISH (1 hour 15 minutes)

Part 1

For questions **1–8**, read the text below and decide which answer (**A**, **B**, **C** or **D**) best fits each gap. There is an example at the beginning (**0**).

Mark your answers **on the separate answer sheet**.

Example:

0 **A** arrive **B** enter **C** gain **D** stay

0	A	B	C	D
	o	●	o	o

Seeing Australia's most famous animals

Many international visitors to Australia **(0)** .... the country through the city of Melbourne and **(1)** .... out on their tours from there. If you do so, it's extremely **(2)** .... that you will ever **(3)** .... across kangaroos or koalas in the city. You'll have to get out of town to see them. You can always book a tour that **(4)** .... wildlife watching experiences.

On the other hand, you may decide to do it on your own. In that case, head out on the Great Ocean Road from Melbourne and you'll see the Kennett River Holiday Park. You'll soon find loads of koalas in the trees. After your **(5)** .... there, drive up to the Grampians National Park. It's **(6)** .... worth taking an afternoon walk there before renting a room at the Kookaburra Lodge looking out on the stunning scenery. Kangaroos **(7)** .... in large groups at sunrise and sunset, and you'll have a front **(8)** .... seat.

1	**A** leave	**B** carry	**C** set	**D** break
2	**A** unknown	**B** unclear	**C** uncertain	**D** unlikely
3	**A** come	**B** bring	**C** get	**D** look
4	**A** deals	**B** offers	**C** specialises	**D** focuses
5	**A** incident	**B** occasion	**C** instance	**D** time
6	**A** just	**B** simply	**C** well	**D** deeply
7	**A** blend	**B** gather	**C** attend	**D** combine
8	**A** place	**B** row	**C** queue	**D** line

→ p. 109

Part 2

For questions **9–16**, read the text below and think of the word which best fits each gap. Use only **one** word in each gap. There is an example at the beginning (**0**).

Write your answers **IN CAPITAL LETTERS on the separate answer sheet**.

Example: | 0 | | *I* | *N* |

The Oscars

Many countries have annual awards for outstanding achievements **(0)** .... the film industry. By **(9)** .... the most famous awards are those made by the American Academy of Motion Picture Arts and Sciences – the Oscars. The name actually refers **(10)** .... the statuette which all of the winners receive. The awards go not only to actors but also to other people involved in the production of a film, **(11)** .... as make-up artists and costume designers.

Nobody knows for certain **(12)** .... these statuettes are called Oscars. The most widely accepted story concerns Margaret Herrick, the secretary to the Academy. **(13)** .... she first saw the statuettes in 1931, her initial reaction **(14)** .... to say that they looked remarkably **(15)** .... her cousin, Oscar Pierce. He worked on a farm and actually had **(16)** .... at all to do with the film industry.

 → p. 109

Part 3

For questions **17–24**, read the text below. Use the word given in capitals at the end of some of the lines to form a word that fits in the gap **in the same line**. There is an example at the beginning (**0**).

Write your answers **IN CAPITAL LETTERS on the separate answer sheet**.

Example: | 0 | I | N | F | L | U | E | N | T | I | A | L |

Drawing with scissors

Frenchman Henri Matisse was among the most **(0)** .... artists	**INFLUENCE**
of the twentieth century. He produced masterpieces in a wide	
(17) .... of media including painting, sculpture and printmaking,	**VARY**
but some consider his most **(18)** .... work to be from his	**INNOVATE**
later years, when he suffered from partial **(19)** .... and was	**BLIND**
confined to his bed and a wheelchair. Because of this, he used an	
(20) .... method he called 'drawing with scissors'. He cut brightly-	**EXPERIMENT**
painted sheets of paper into large shapes. Under his guidance these	
paper cut-outs were attached to the walls of his studio. He then	
directed his **(21)** .... to move the pieces into the precise	**ASSIST**
(22) .... he had in mind.	**ARRANGE**
The inspiration for some of the most remarkable scissor drawings	
was **(23)** .... places Matisse had previously visited but, because	**MEMORY**
of his age, could no longer return to, such as two works he made in	
1946 based on an **(24)** .... trip he had made to Tahiti many years	**FORGET**
before.	

→ p. 109

Part 4

For questions **25–30**, complete the second sentence so that it has a similar meaning to the first sentence, using the word given. **Do not change the word given**. You must use between **two** and **five** words, including the word given. Here is an example (**0**).

Example:

0 A very friendly taxi driver drove us into town.

DRIVEN

We .... a very friendly taxi driver.

The gap can be filled by the words 'were driven into town by', so you write:

Example:	**0**	*WERE DRIVEN INTO TOWN BY*

Write **only** the missing words **IN CAPITAL LETTERS on the separate answer sheet.**

---

25 I cannot remember a time when Dr Rowan was not the president of the club.

AS

Dr Rowan has been the president of the club for .... remember.

26 The furthest my brother can run is 5 kilometres.

NO

My brother .... 5 kilometres.

27 I spent more money on my holiday than I meant to.

SO

I didn't .... money on my holiday.

28 My doctor said that I must only run in proper running shoes.

NEVER

My doctor told .... I was wearing proper running shoes.

29 The engineer explained clearly how the machinery worked.

CLEAR

The engineer gave a .... how the machinery worked.

30 The concert was cancelled when it began to snow.

OWING

The concert was called .... the snow.

→ p. 109

Part 5

You are going to read an extract from the autobiography of the tennis player Rafael Nadal. For questions **31–36**, choose the answer (**A**, **B**, **C** or **D**) which you think fits best according to the text.

Mark your answers **on the separate answer sheet**.

Looking back at the Wimbledon tennis championships

The silence, that's what strikes you when you play on Centre Court at the Wimbledon tennis championships. You bounce the ball soundlessly up and down on the soft grass surface; you toss it up to serve; you hit it and you hear the echo of your own shot. And of every shot after that. The trimmed grass, the rich history, the ancient stadium, the players dressed in white, the respectful crowds, all combine to enclose and cushion you from the outside world. The quiet of the Centre Court is good for my game. What I battle against hardest in a tennis match is to shut everything out of my mind but the contest itself and the point I'm playing.

The silence of the Centre Court is broken by a shock of noise when a point's done: applause, cheers, people shouting your name. I hear them, but as if from some place far off. I don't register that there are fifteen thousand people hunched around the arena, tracking every move my opponent and I make. I am so focused I have no sense at all that there are millions watching me around the world as I play Roger Federer in the 2008 Wimbledon final – the biggest match of my life.

I had always dreamed of playing at Wimbledon. My uncle Toni, who has been my coach all my life, had drummed into me from an early age that this was the biggest tournament of them all. By the time I was 14, I was sharing with my friends the fantasy that I'd play there one day and win. Before 2008, though, I'd played and lost, both times against Federer – in the final there the year before, and the year before that. The defeat in 2006 had not been so hard. I went out onto the court that time just pleased and grateful that, having just turned twenty, I'd made it that far. Federer beat me pretty easily, more easily than if I'd gone out with more belief. But my defeat in 2007 left me utterly destroyed. I knew I could have done better, that it was not my ability or the quality of my game that had failed me, but my head. Losing always hurts, but it hurts much more when you have a chance and throw it away.

Toni, the toughest of tennis coaches, is usually the last person in the world to offer me consolation; he criticizes me even when I win. It is a measure of what a wreck I must have been that he abandoned the habit of a lifetime and told me there was no reason to despair, that there would be more Wimbledons and more Wimbledon finals. I told him he didn't understand, that this had probably been my last chance to win it. Every single moment counts but some moments count for more than others, and I had let a big one pass in 2007.

There was nothing Toni could do to ease my grief. Yet here I was again in 2008, just one year later. I was confident I'd learnt the lesson from that defeat twelve months earlier; that whatever else gave way this time, my head would not. The best sign that my head was in the right place now was the conviction that I would win.

At dinner with family and friends and team members the night before the final, at the house we always rent when I play at Wimbledon, mention of the match had been off-limits. I didn't expressly forbid them from raising the subject, but they all understood well enough that, whatever else I might have been talking about, I was already beginning to play the match in a space inside my head. From here on in until the start of play, that space should remain mine alone.

31 The writer says that the silence at Wimbledon Centre Court

A calms his nerves during matches.
B gives him confidence in his abilities.
C helps him to concentrate on the game.
D makes him feel that he's respected.

32 In the second paragraph, what does the writer suggest about the 2008 match?

A It was all that concerned him at that time.
B His opponent was distracted by the behaviour of the crowd.
C It proved how popular he had become.
D His fans seemed almost as anxious as he was.

33 What does the writer say about playing Federer in two Wimbledon finals?

A Nerves let him down in the first match.
B He had different attitudes to the two matches.
C He was too ambitious when he played the first match.
D The quality of his game improved in the second match.

34 The writer says that after he lost in the 2007 final, his coach

A encouraged him to think about how much he'd already achieved.
B was unusually sympathetic towards him.
C failed to recognise his disappointment.
D criticised his performance unfairly.

35 What does 'gave way' mean in line 65?

A developed unexpectedly
B became stronger
C kept going through difficulties
D failed to function

36 What does the writer say about his family and friends?

A They take his mind off tennis.
B They respect his need for privacy.
C They help him in any way they can.
D They see things from a different perspective.

→ p. 109

Part 6

You are going to read a magazine article about video games. Six sentences have been removed from the article. Choose from the sentences **A–G** the one which fits each gap (**37–42**). There is one extra sentence which you do not need to use.

Mark your answers **on the separate answer sheet.**

In praise of video games

Why do serious media commentators largely ignore the biggest entertainment medium in the world? Author Naomi Alderman investigates.

Why do video games receive so little coverage in the mainstream media? It's a question that's troubled me for years – I even made a programme about it for the radio. Games are the largest entertainment medium in the world, yet newspaper culture pages tend not to cover them. Cultural programmes on TV and radio might do a short feature about them once in a while at best, reserving serious discussion and analysis for specialist things with a very limited audience like interpretive dance and experimental opera.

My novels, which sell tens of thousands of copies, are shortlisted for prizes that appear on the news. My games, which have sold millions of copies, don't even make the news. Film and TV awards ceremonies are a news story. **37** I think all this is a shame because it affects the way people think about the medium. It means we don't get the kind of analysis that mainstream media can produce, and we're prevented from asking interesting questions about games in our culture.

There are several reasons for this exclusion. People who control programming and edit papers tend to be in their 50s and older, and are still a bit old to have come of age with video games or to understand them. And games, because they're very much products of a collaborative effort, normally don't have a single creator or celebrity to represent them in interviews. **38**

But I want to suggest another reason why games aren't treated as an important cultural form. **39** At least, that is the impression I get. They make it amazingly hard to get hold of new games, even for someone who writes about them.

I write about novels as well as games and barely a day passes when a publisher isn't posting me a copy of a new book in the hope I'll review it or mention it somewhere. **40** If the games industry wanted to be treated like other cultural media, it could start by making its work accessible to mainstream journalists.

There's a timing issue too. In the past, I've tried to persuade review programmes to cover games more frequently. But I always seem to come up against the same old problem. Film companies organise pre-release screenings, TV companies send out early versions of their shows, publishers send copies of new books, theatres do previews – but games companies won't send out advance versions of games. **41**

Furthermore, the games industry itself does not seem too bothered about being covered in broadsheet culture sections, because it doesn't think this would sell more games. It is already the biggest selling entertainment industry in the world in any case. **42** It's a fair point, but I wish the industry would cooperate anyway because games are important and deserve to be regarded as such in the mainstream media.

A With books you have authors; with films you have directors; so the situation is very different.

B However, gamers are still being viewed as socially inadequate teenagers.

C So what difference would, for example, a weekly games programme on TV make to it?

D Those for games are only for industry specialists.

E This is that the people in the games industry itself don't care enough.

F That's because they usually need to make technical changes right up until the last minute.

G By contrast, I spend hours doing phone-rounds in the hope of getting hold of a copy of a game.

→ p. 109

Part 7

You are going to read an article written by an architect about his work. For questions **43–52**, choose from the sections (**A–D**). The sections may be chosen more than once.

Mark your answers **on the separate answer sheet**.

In which section does the architect mention

employees being trusted to organise themselves in the way they think is best?	**43**	
how problems among employees are resolved?	**44**	
the range of people needed for some architectural projects?	**45**	
being told that he would have fewer responsibilities in a new position?	**46**	
the limited control higher-ranking people have over what employees do?	**47**	
seeking help from colleagues?	**48**	
having mixed feelings about his work?	**49**	
a requirement for the performance of all employees to be exceptional?	**50**	
the value of employees to his business?	**51**	
having to demonstrate independence straightaway in a new post?	**52**	

 → p. 109

Being an architect

A After I graduated, I took the first job I was offered. I felt torn at the time because although I was really happy to have found a job right out of school when so many others could not, I hated retail design at architectural school and this was a firm specialising in retail stores. It was a small company (I was the first employee hired) and because it did work around the country, my boss travelled quite a bit. Almost from day one, I was left on my own for several days a week and, through necessity, I was taking meetings with local clients and giving presentations without help. It wasn't too much later that I started helping with the billing and managing some of the proposal writing duties. I got to do it all. When I left the job, I remember going into an interview with a larger firm and telling them that I had all this experience. The person interviewing me chuckled and said, 'You won't be doing that here straightaway – that's what the senior employees do.'

B I now run my own small company. Because we're not so big, we really need everyone in the office to be superstars. It can be a difficult environment for some types of people to work in because we expect everyone to work on their own initiative. We need our employees to make the most of the resources available to them, including asking questions of others on their team, looking at past projects and using the lessons learned to find possible ways forward. We give our staff plenty of time and space to do their own thing. They need to be clever enough to arrange and make use of this time and space wisely.

C Everybody in our office is part of a team. Normally, we have two or three people working on a project, and everybody has access to the same people and information. Individuals tend to roll on and off projects as and when needed. There is always a senior level person who remains on a project throughout the entire process and is the point of contact, but we like to let people find their own roles on projects and pursue the things that interest them. We all get along pretty well and any issues with behaviour get dealt with as they arise between the individuals concerned. The people who work for me really are the company's most important asset. Sure, we could replace them with others, but it would be very hard to find the right balance of skills that we currently have.

D I often get asked if architecture is a field for everyone. It's a difficult question to answer. What I look for in potential new employees is their ability to speak articulately. This is essential. Since we require all employees to meet with clients, they need to be able to construct a narrative that can engage our clients and which they can relate to. I look for the same characteristics in all employees, regardless of gender, nationality, age, whatever. I think it takes a certain type of brain to practise architecture but that doesn't necessarily mean that everyone can't find a place. While most people don't go into architectural school thinking that they are going to be anything other than the world's next great designer, the truth of the matter is that it takes a small army of people from diverse backgrounds to take on some of the buildings being constructed these days.

WRITING (1 hour 20 minutes)

Part 1

You **must** answer this question. Write your answer in **140–190** words in an appropriate style on the separate answer sheet.

---

1 In your English class you have been talking about helping other people. Now, your English teacher has asked you to write an essay.

Write your essay using **all** the notes and giving reasons for your point of view.

'Everyone should do something regularly in their life to help other people.' Do you agree?

Notes

Write about:

1. the importance of friends and family
2. giving something back to society
3. .... (your own idea)

 → p. 100

Part 2

Write an answer to **one** of the questions **2–4** in this part. Write your answer in **140–190** words in an appropriate style on the separate answer sheet. Put the question number in the box at the top of the answer sheet.

---

2 Your English teacher has asked you to write a report on the cycling facilities in your area for the college magazine.
In your report, you should:

- explain what facilities are available for cyclists
- describe popular places for cyclists to visit
- recommend ways in which cycling can be made safer in your area.

Write your **report**.

3 You have seen this announcement in an English-language magazine.

> **Articles wanted**
>
> **A sense of humour**
>
> What does having a good sense of humour mean? How important is it to see the funny side of life? Are there any disadvantages to laughing a lot?
>
> The best articles will be published in our magazine.

Write your **article**.

4 You receive this email from your English friend, Hannah.

> **Subject:** Summer job
>
> I want to get a job in the summer. My uncle works for a publishing company and says I could work there. It'd be really interesting but they can't afford to pay me much. Or I could work in the local supermarket. The pay would be better but it'd be really boring. What should I do?

Write your **email**.

→ p. 102

LISTENING (approximately 40 minutes)

Listening test audio

Part 1

You will hear people talking in eight different situations.
For questions **1–8**, choose the best answer (**A**, **B** or **C**).

---

1 You hear a woman talking about learning to play the piano.

How does she feel about it?

A determined not to give up

B disappointed at her lack of progress

C embarrassed that she rarely practises

2 You hear a woman telling a friend about having a celebration dinner.

How does the woman feel about it?

A proud of the meal that she prepared

B pleased that everyone enjoyed the evening

C relieved that there was enough to eat

3 You hear a man telling a friend about a visit to a museum.

What does he say about the visit?

A It inspired him to take up a hobby.

B It was more interesting than he'd expected.

C It would have been more enjoyable on another day.

4 You hear two media students talking about a TV advert they have seen.

What do they agree about the advert?

A It was cleverly made.

B It was harmless fun.

C It was aimed at a particular age group.

5 You hear two people talking about a work colleague called Judy.

What is the man doing when he speaks?

A praising Judy's enthusiasm

B questioning Judy's attention to detail

C expressing sympathy for Judy

6 You hear two friends talking about a local project to start a community garden.

What does the man think about the project?

A It seems badly organised.

B It's probably over-ambitious.

C It risks being too costly.

7 You hear two friends discussing watching films based on books.

The woman enjoys watching films based on books she's read because

A the book brings an added level of understanding to the film.

B it is interesting to see another interpretation of the story.

C she likes to spot where the film differs from the book.

8 You hear a man telling a friend about a new sports centre.

For which sport is it optional to join a membership scheme?

A swimming

B gym

C athletics

→ p. 110 p. 111

Part 2

You will hear a student called Petra Dean talking about her recent work experience as a volunteer in the Cloud Forest in Ecuador in South America. For questions **9–18**, complete the sentences with a word or short phrase.

Listening test audio

Volunteering in the Ecuadorian Cloud Forest

Petra is currently studying **(9)** .... at university.

Petra was surprised that she had to travel by **(10)** .... for the last stage of her journey to the Cloud Forest.

Working in what was known as the **(11)** .... gave Petra particular satisfaction.

Petra was impressed by the **(12)** .... she saw on a daily basis.

Petra didn't enjoy trying to control the **(13)** .... when taking the milk down the mountain.

As part of the forest programme, Petra had to check the

(14) .... of the trees.

One survival skill that Petra learnt was how to make

(15) .... in the trees.

Visiting **(16)** .... that are now in a state of ruin was Petra's most memorable free time activity.

In the reserve, Petra's favourite place to spend the evening was the

(17) ....

Petra regretted not packing sufficient **(18)** .... in her luggage.

 → p. 110 p. 115

Part 3

You will hear five short extracts in which people talk about their jobs on a cruise ship. For questions **19–23**, choose from the list (**A–H**) what each speaker says about working on a cruise ship. Use the letters only once. There are three extra letters which you do not need to use.

Listening test audio

A The staff can choose which cruise to go on.

B The staff tend to be young.

C The jobs are well paid.

D The staff can continue their education on board.

E The promotion prospects are good.

F The staff accommodation is of a high standard.

G The lifestyle is glamorous.

H The work is suitable for couples.

Speaker 1		**19**
Speaker 2		**20**
Speaker 3		**21**
Speaker 4		**22**
Speaker 5		**23**

→ p. 110 p. 117

Part 4

You will hear an interview with a man called Guy Riordan, who works as a stuntman performing dangerous scenes in movies. For questions **24–30**, choose the best answer (**A**, **B** or **C**).

Listening test audio

---

24 What does Guy say about the first time he worked with a team of other stuntmen?

A He was very unsure of his talents.

B He was uncomfortable about putting his trust in others.

C He was surprised at the risks some people took.

25 For Guy, the most difficult part of being a stuntman is

A competing against others for roles.

B avoiding injury.

C trying to improve constantly.

26 What does Guy say was hard about performing in the movie *Raw Stuff*?

A falling in the right place

B having to carry heavy loads

C getting to the top of a mountain

27 When asked about being a stunt double for the actor Marty Walker, Guy says

A he admires Marty's ability to change his body shape for films.

B he feels pleased when Marty plays the parts of action heroes.

C he respects Marty's willingness to act in some dangerous scenes.

28 What was satisfying for Guy about performing in the film *Light at Dawn*?

A getting the chance to have a speaking role

B working with a large film crew

C achieving what the director wanted

29 What has changed for Guy about the movie industry recently?

A People working in it are more serious than before.

B He has to do more work for the same money.

C Stunt performers are less frequently required.

30 Guy advises anyone interested in becoming a movie stunt performer

A to develop as wide a range of stunt skills as possible.

B to find jobs by using a good agent.

C to be prepared to do other types of work as well.

→ p. 110 p. 119

Test 2

READING AND USE OF ENGLISH (1 hour 15 minutes)

Part 1

For questions **1–8**, read the text below and decide which answer (**A**, **B**, **C** or **D**) best fits each gap. There is an example at the beginning (**0**).

Mark your answers **on the separate answer sheet**.

Example:

0 **A** regard **B** think **C** agree **D** believe

0	A	B	C	D
	●	o	o	o

Aspects of character

Psychologists **(0)** .... introversion and extroversion as highly important aspects of character. Extroverts are lively and outgoing, while introverts are more controlled and reserved. People who are total extroverts may be rather irritating at times as they always seem to want to be the **(1)** .... of attention, whilst introverts can seem rather dull and boring because they are so quiet. Of course, very few people are totally extrovert or totally introvert; most fall somewhere between the two extremes, some **(2)** .... to extroversion, others to introversion.

The **(3)** .... to which a person is extroverted or introverted can be very relevant to a person's **(4)** .... for a particular job. Some jobs **(5)** .... people who are somewhat extrovert (sales, public relations), other jobs are more appropriate for people with a **(6)** .... to introversion (computer programming, librarianship). For this reason, companies looking to **(7)** .... new staff will often give applicants a psychometric test to see, amongst other things, where they lie on the introversion–extroversion **(8)** ....

1	**A**	centre	**B**	aim	**C**	middle	**D**	point
2	**A**	approaching	**B**	inclining	**C**	moving	**D**	directing
3	**A**	amount	**B**	rate	**C**	level	**D**	extent
4	**A**	suitability	**B**	competency	**C**	adequacy	**D**	capability
5	**A**	expect	**B**	search	**C**	require	**D**	appeal
6	**A**	trend	**B**	custom	**C**	preference	**D**	tendency
7	**A**	find out	**B**	get up	**C**	take on	**D**	show in
8	**A**	scale	**B**	category	**C**	series	**D**	range

→ p. 121

Part 2

For questions **9–16**, read the text below and think of the word which best fits each gap. Use only **one** word in each gap. There is an example at the beginning (**0**).

Write your answers **IN CAPITAL LETTERS on the separate answer sheet**.

Example: | 0 | *T H E* |

Nordic walking

Nordic walking is an outdoor activity first developed in **(0)** .... 1930s in Finland. It basically involves walking with very light sticks a bit like ski-poles, **(9)** .... are strapped to your wrists and used to push you along.

Nordic walking was initially devised **(10)** .... a form of summer exercise for winter cross-country skiers, but was not taken seriously for general fitness training until roughly the turn **(11)** .... the century. Since then, **(12)** .... popularity has exploded in Europe, and it is taking **(13)** .... in the USA, Australia and Japan.

The appeal of the activity is obvious. Not **(14)** .... is it easy to do, but Nordic walking is apparently the most complete body workout there is, using more muscles than either running or swimming. For people who dislike gyms, it is perfect. Nordic walking can be done almost **(15)** ...., from beaches and parks **(16)** .... city streets.

 → p. 121

Part 3

For questions **17–24**, read the text below. Use the word given in capitals at the end of some of the lines to form a word that fits in the gap **in the same line**. There is an example at the beginning (**0**).

Write your answers **IN CAPITAL LETTERS on the separate answer sheet**.

Example: | 0 | P | R | O | F | E | S | S | I | O | N | A | L |

Canadian astronaut

Chris Hadfield was the first **(0)** .... astronaut from Canada to	**PROFESS**
travel in **(17)** .... space. He says that his inspiration for wanting	**OUT**
to be an astronaut came when, at the age of just nine, he and his	
family watched the first moon **(18)** .... in July, 1969 at their home	**LAND**
in Ontario. Chris never lost **(19)** .... of this ambition throughout his	**SEE**
(20)	**BOY**
Then, at the age of 18, he went on to study mechanical engineering	
and later aviation studies. In 1992, after serving as a test pilot for	
several years, he was chosen from over 5,000 **(21)** .... who	**APPLY**
wanted to join the Canadian space programme. He then had to	
undergo a training programme which was extremely **(22)** .... both	**RIGOUR**
physically and mentally.	
He was selected for his first space **(23)** .... in 1995 on the US	**FLY**
space shuttle *Atlantis*. He served on several different types of	
space mission, and was appointed to the role of **(24)** .... of the	**COMMAND**
International Space Station mission in 2013.	

→ p. 121

Part 4

For questions **25–30**, complete the second sentence so that it has a similar meaning to the first sentence, using the word given. **Do not change the word given**. You must use between **two** and **five** words, including the word given. Here is an example (**0**).

Example:

0 A very friendly taxi driver drove us into town.

DRIVEN

We .... a very friendly taxi driver.

The gap can be filled by the words 'were driven into town by', so you write:

Example:	**0**	*WERE DRIVEN INTO TOWN BY*

Write **only** the missing words **IN CAPITAL LETTERS on the separate answer sheet.**

---

25 Steven asked me, 'Do you want to go to the movies with me?'

LIKE

Steven asked me .... go to the movies with him.

26 Philip told Maria he would contact her on Saturday.

TOUCH

Philip promised Maria he would .... her on Saturday.

27 My sister said she would help me do my homework.

HAND

My sister offered to .... with my homework.

28 We didn't get to sleep at all last night because of the noise from the room next door.

IMPOSSIBLE

The noise from the room next door .... us to get to sleep last night.

29 Would you like to come shopping this afternoon?

FEEL

Do you .... this afternoon?

30 It was hard for me to understand what the visitor was saying.

DIFFICULTY

I .... what the visitor was saying.

→ p. 121

Part 5

You are going to read an extract from the biography of a biologist called Jane Goodall. For questions **31–36**, choose the answer (**A**, **B**, **C** or **D**) which you think fits best according to the text.

Mark your answers **on the separate answer sheet**.

Jane Goodall: chimpanzee expert

A very young, idealistic Englishwoman arrived in Africa in early April 1957 and soon, quite possibly in her first letter home, wrote the astonishingly dramatic words 'I am living in the Africa I have always longed for, always felt stirring in my blood.' She was to spend most of the rest of her life in Africa and – as a citizen, journalist, scientist, activist and environmentalist – came to be associated with that continent. Her name was Jane Goodall.

In 1963, Britain's National Geographical Society promoted Jane Goodall's fame by producing a series of glossy articles and television documentaries on her chimpanzee research. That early fame has since been reinforced by her own writing for a popular audience, including award-winning children's books and the 1971 bestseller *In the Shadow of Man*, which has been translated into 47 languages and is still in print. With the possible exception of Marie Curie, the Nobel Prize-winning scientist, Jane Goodall must be the most widely celebrated female scientist of the 20th century.

Ironically, her celebrity may have obscured her actual achievements. Hundreds of articles, interviews and books have told her life story but they are often limited in scope and sentimental. She has been presented as an adventure-seeking little girl, a privileged woman who dreamed of a life with wild animals, a determined feminist in a man's world, and so on. Put together, these images devalue what she has actually done. Based on the number of references to her research by academics in her field, the number of her students who have subsequently reached influential positions in the biological sciences, and the volume of data amassed in her forty-year-long study, Jane Goodall ought to be considered a uniquely distinguished pioneer in her field and the world's leading zoologist. Yet her achievement can be stated more simply and directly: she opened the door to our understanding of the social and emotional lives of chimpanzees.

Wild chimpanzees are dangerous, though before Goodall began her work the dangers were misunderstood and exaggerated. Prior to Goodall's early discoveries, no one knew that chimpanzees ate meat. We had no idea that they, or indeed any large mammals other than ourselves, created and used tools. We did not realize that chimpanzees share with humans a similar set of emotions or that their social systems are startlingly like ours. We would not have believed that chimpanzee communities across Africa possess various distinctive cultural traditions.

Goodall's scholarly book, *The Chimpanzees of Gombe* (1986), ranks as the single most authoritative work in this area, the first encyclopaedia for chimpanzee research. Her long-term study of wild apes along the shores of Lake Tanganyika in Gombe State, Nigeria, has turned out to be, in the words of biologist Stephen Jay Gould, 'one of the Western world's great scientific achievements'. Jane Goodall helped create a revolution in the way we study animals, and because the animals she studied are humankind's closest relatives, she also helped alter the way humans think about themselves.

Even as a child, there were a few early indicators of the person Jane Goodall would become. By far the clearest of these from her early childhood was in the autumn of 1939, when she was just five years old. One autumn day, a 'golden afternoon' as her mother remembers it, Jane disappeared. The police were called and began the search. Neighbours and family members joined in. After an increasingly frantic search, as dusk moved to dark, the child suddenly reappeared, alone, with fragments of straw in her hair and clothes. 'Wherever have you been?' her mother asked. Jane explained that she had wondered how hens lay eggs. To find out, she had crawled inside a henhouse, concealed herself in the straw, and lain perfectly still for five hours until the hen raised herself up, wiggled and provided an answer. It is tempting to consider this as the beginning of her career as a biologist.

31 In the first paragraph, we learn that Goodall

A had been wanting to travel to Africa for some time.
B recognised that she was unusual in wanting to go to Africa.
C initially felt limited by the job she was doing.
D sometimes found it difficult to express herself in writing.

32 Goodall's book *In the Shadow of Man* is mentioned to make the point that

A she contributed to the spread of her own fame.
B she tried her best to compete with other female scientists.
C she was interested in collaborating with scientists abroad.
D she was more interested in books than television programmes.

33 What is the writer doing in the third paragraph?

A questioning some of the decisions Goodall made
B describing the many sides of Goodall's personality
C emphasising the significance of Goodall's work
D arguing that most books on Goodall are well researched

34 What does the writer say about Goodall's book *The Chimpanzees of Gombe*?

A The importance of it was not immediately obvious.
B There is no better book on the subject.
C It inspired a leading scientist to write a similar book.
D It encouraged other biologists to visit Lake Tanganyika.

35 What is the writer's purpose in telling the story about the hen?

A to give an example of the imaginative games Goodall played
B to point out how unusual Goodall's interests were
C to show how different Goodall's character was as a child
D to highlight Goodall's intellectual curiosity

36 What does 'provided an answer' (line 87) refer to?

A the question her mother asked
B Goodall's curiosity
C Goodall's actions
D the search for Goodall

→ p. 121

Part 6

You are going to read an article which compares performing stand-up comedy with giving a presentation. Six sentences have been removed from the article. Choose from the sentences **A–G** the one which fits each gap (**37–42**). There is one extra sentence which you do not need to use.

Mark your answers **on the separate answer sheet.**

Stand-up comedy and presentations

Monica Platter describes how her experiences on a stage performing stand-up comedy helped her to get better at giving presentations for work.

I work in marketing, but I've always fancied trying stand-up comedy in my spare time. Earlier this year, I finally plucked up courage and made a series of appearances on stage at a comedy club. The experience provided me with some useful lessons for the public speaking I do in my normal job.

To start with, half an hour trying to be funny on stage is a long time. The first five minutes are normally fine, just as the start of a work presentation usually goes well. But then a rather awkward 25 minutes often follow. I tend to speak very quickly and run out of things to say, but after a couple of difficult experiences at the club I realised I needed to speak at half the speed. That way I immediately made life easier for myself. **37** I've subsequently tried to slow down in the presentations I give at work, and it's definitely helped.

I also learned that you shouldn't judge your performance by the audience's reaction. If they aren't laughing, it doesn't necessarily mean they don't think it's funny. It could just be that they aren't laughers. Similarly, in a presentation, if your audience isn't looking excited, it might just be that they don't show much emotion. You might have been good or rubbish up to that point. **38** Do that and you'll end up feeling better.

Every comedian I met at the club said that knowing how to pause is crucial. **39** They get the joke and wait in suspense to find out what comes next. I've realised that the same principle applies to other types of public speaking. It's good to extend your pauses and use them to make your listeners think before you move on.

Another thing I noticed was that even comedians who seem very confident are mostly just good at appearing confident. I would often stand at the club almost fainting with fear, but I managed to deliver a routine that people thought was calm and polished. **40** If you appear to be in control, however, people believe that you know what you're doing, and they listen to you. It's true of other public speaking too.

Then, there is the use of fillers, techniques that comedians and public speakers regularly employ. I've seen some take a sip of water, while others adjust the microphone lead, even though they're not thirsty and the microphone sounds fine. **41** So, whether you're going to do stand-up or business talks, develop fillers that you feel comfortable with.

The bottom line with stand-up comedians, however, is that it's always been about performance and delivery. Everything I saw at the club confirmed that. **42** I've been to great shows where 80% of the humour came from the comedian's facial expressions, and eyebrow movements seem particularly important. I've been focussing on improving my eyebrow use when I'm giving work presentations. I'm still not as good as I'd like, but I'm making progress, and much of this is down to what I've learned from stand-up.

A It felt more like a shaky mess to me than anything else, to be honest.

B This showed the importance of observing your audience and responding to them.

C This told me the best script in the world is nothing in the hands of someone who isn't funny in themselves.

D It just provides them with an opportunity to remember what they were meant to say next.

E Either way, the best thing to do is carry on and assume they're really getting a lot out of it.

F It was a major turning point for me.

G It's when your audience has a think about what you've just said.

→ p. 121

Part 7

You are going to read a magazine article about a form of art called Ebru. For questions **43–52**, choose from the sections (**A–E**). The sections may be chosen more than once.

Mark your answers **on the separate answer sheet**.

In which section does the writer

say that the final design is exactly the same as the one created on the water?	**43**	
claim that Ebru is a combination of ancient and modern art?	**44**	
suggest that the results of using the Ebru technique can be unpredictable?	**45**	
identify the mental attitude an artist should have when working on Ebru?	**46**	
explain ways in which one substance is vital to Ebru?	**47**	
mention that Ebru is expanding into new genres of painting?	**48**	
reveal how knowledge of the Ebru technique has been kept alive?	**49**	
claim there is a link between colour and feelings?	**50**	
mention what the original subject of Ebru painting was?	**51**	
give an example of the way different shades of paint can be used in Ebru?	**52**	

 → p. 121

The fascinating art of Ebru

A The art of Ebru can produce stunning results. It involves painting on the surface of water, then transferring the moving image to paper or fabric. The results are spectacular – strikingly contemporary, yet rooted in the tradition of a centuries-old art form. There are two key ingredients: tragacanth, a soft gum which makes the water more dense, and ox gall. The ox gall has two essential properties: first, it allows colours to float and spread on the surface of the water; second, it prevents the colour from merging or simply dissolving.

B An Ebru artist, Hayrettin Kozanoglu, demonstrates by dipping a brush into pots of vivid colours arranged around a shallow rectangular tray of water, then sprinkling paint onto the surface. 'I can drop on green, then blue on top, then add yellow, and the colours stay completely separate,' he says. He takes a small comb and swirls it across the surface. Instead of the colours merging into a muddy mess, as would happen with oil or acrylic paint, the tray fills with swirling curly designs of the kind seen inside the front and back covers of old hardback books. Finally, Kozanoglu places a piece of paper onto the tray, carefully presses it flat without submerging it, then deftly slides it out. The pattern he created in the tray has been transferred to the sheet with absolute precision.

C Prior to arriving in Europe in the 17th century, a similar art form to Ebru had developed across Asia. A 10th-century Chinese book mentions 'drifting sand notepaper' made by dragging paper through a fermented flour paste mixed with colours, while *suminagashi*, or 'floating ink', was known in 12th-century Japan. By the 15th century, India and countries across central Asia had their own indigenous versions. The current Turkish tradition of Ebru dates to the mid-19th century and the work of several masters, who passed on their skills to apprentices.

D Ebru artists are renowned for intricate depictions of flowers, as well as abstract patterns. Kozanoglu explains that the technique is evolving: 'Before the 20th century, it was only about flowers. As more people are learning about Ebru, interesting experiments are happening. Artists are creating landscapes and even portraits – although it takes many years of practice to reach that level. The beauty of Ebru is that you can create attractive and complex works of art quickly and easily. Ebru has the potential to surprise us because the water and paint permit new and exciting things to happen.'

E Kozanoglu recognises the therapeutic value of Ebru in helping people with emotional problems: 'To make Ebru art, you need to concentrate, to be calm and patient. Also, the colours you choose can be a reflection of your personality, your mood and your circumstances. Water is the source of life and I believe it holds memories. That's why the way in which people make the connection between the water and the paint is important.' It's an art form that gives pleasure to the many people who practise it – and also recognition of the power of water in helping to create a more colourful and inspiring world.

WRITING (1 hour 20 minutes)

Part 1

You **must** answer this question. Write your answer in **140–190** words in an appropriate style on the separate answer sheet.

---

1 In your English class you have been talking about sport. Now, your English teacher has asked you to write an essay.

Write your essay using **all** the notes and giving reasons for your point of view.

'All students should have to do sport at school.'
Do you agree?

Notes

Write about:

1. learning teamwork
2. some people hate sport
3. .... (your own idea)

 → p. 103

Part 2

Write an answer to **one** of the questions **2–4** in this part. Write your answer in **140–190** words in an appropriate style on the separate answer sheet. Put the question number in the box at the top of the answer sheet.

---

2 You have been on a week's course to improve your speaking and listening skills in English. Now your teacher has asked you to write a report about your experience.

In your report, you should:

- say when and where the course took place
- describe what you did during the course
- recommend any improvements you think could be made to the course.

Write your **report**.

3 You have seen this notice in an English-language magazine.

> **Articles wanted**
>
> **Useful advice**
>
> What is the most useful advice you have ever been given? Write us an article explaining what the advice was. Why was it so useful to you and what effect has it had on your life?
>
> The best articles will be published in our magazine.

Write your **article**.

4 You have seen this advertisement online.

> **Wanted – Tourist Website Designer**
>
> We are looking for someone to design a tourist website for your local area. Write to Adam Jones, Tourist Officer, explaining why you are suitable for the job.
> You should:
> - have good knowledge of your local area
> - be interested in web design
> - be able to communicate well in English.

Write your **letter of application**.

→ p. 104

LISTENING (approximately 40 minutes)

Part 1

Listening test audio

You will hear people talking in eight different situations.
For questions **1–8**, choose the best answer (**A**, **B** or **C**).

---

1 You hear a TV presenter talking about making travel documentaries for TV.

What does he appreciate most about his job?

A It allows him plenty of free time.

B It doesn't feel like work.

C It provides him with a good salary.

2 You hear an interview with a woman talking about rowing across the Atlantic Ocean.

How did she and her team feel before they set out?

A concerned that their age would be a problem

B worried about the weather conditions at sea

C unsure that they would complete the journey

3 You hear two colleagues talking about what they did at the weekend.

How did the woman spend her time?

A applying for a new position

B catching up on her work

C improving her job prospects

4 You hear an interview with a musician who is talking about being famous.

What does he enjoy?

A being recognised by the public

B performing in front of an audience

C pretending to be someone he's not

5 You hear part of an interview with a writer in which he talks about the novel he has written.

What does he say about the novel?

A It would make a good film.

B It is a different type of book for him.

C It took him a long time to write.

6 You hear a hotel owner talking about her hotel.

What does she say about the customer service there?

A There is still a lot of room for improvement.

B She researched the subject thoroughly in advance.

C It is typical of the standards she is trying to achieve.

7 You hear two friends talking about a housing development scheme in their town.

The man says that the scheme fails to

A satisfy current housing needs.

B contribute to the local area.

C use all the space available.

8 You hear two people on a discussion programme talking about the way employees dress for work.

What do they agree about?

A A company's image suffers if informal clothes are worn.

B Employers are less concerned about appearance than previously.

C Employees produce better work if they feel more relaxed.

→ p. 122 p. 123

Part 2

You will hear a man called Mark Dawson talking about his visit to the Albuquerque Balloon Festival in New Mexico, USA. For questions **9–18**, complete the sentences with a word or short phrase.

Listening test audio

The Albuquerque Balloon Festival

Mark says **(9)** .... was the month when the Albuquerque Balloon Festival was first held.

Mark found out that the organiser had first used a balloon to promote his

(10) .... firm.

Mark liked the theme of the event this year, which was called

(11) '..'.

Mark says the balloons that have unusual **(12)** .... are the most popular with visitors.

When Mark saw the Flight of Nations balloons, he particularly enjoyed the

(13) .... of different nationalities.

Mark learned that pilots try to find the 'Albuquerque

(14) ....' so they can land in the same place they took off.

Mark says that a balloon is attached by **(15)** ....

to the basket.

Mark was surprised to find out that a pilot sometimes needs to get rid of

(16) .... in order to maintain height.

Mark says that in the bigger balloons, there is a **(17)** .... to protect passengers from the rain.

On the second day of the festival, Mark saw the balloons take off at

(18) ....

→ p. 122 p. 127

Part 3

You will hear five short extracts in which students are talking about starting at university. For questions **19–23**, choose from the list (**A–H**) what each speaker says about how they felt. Use the letters only once. There are three extra letters which you do not need to use.

Listening test audio

A I missed my school friends.

B I was anxious that I might get lost.

C I was excited about meeting new people.

D I felt relieved that I understood the lectures.

E I worried that I'd find the work too difficult.

F I felt confident that I'd chosen the right course.

G I was disappointed by the number of people on my course.

H I was impatient to start my course.

Speaker 1		**19**
Speaker 2		**20**
Speaker 3		**21**
Speaker 4		**22**
Speaker 5		**23**

→ p. 122 p. 129

Part 4

You will hear part of an interview with a marine biologist called Ed Shapiro, who is talking about a diving project in the Pitcairn Islands in the South Pacific. For questions **24–30**, choose the best answer (**A**, **B** or **C**).

Listening test audio

---

24 Ed says that the area his team are currently working in has

A made him feel optimistic about the future.

B escaped the effects of climate change so far.

C exhibited a more limited range of marine life than expected.

25 What happened on Ed's most recent dive?

A He gained further understanding of the reef ecosystem.

B He carried out some different research activities from his colleagues.

C He spent longer than he normally does under water.

26 What does Ed say about using cameras to photograph marine life?

A He is constantly amazed by what photos can reveal.

B He thinks underwater equipment could be improved.

C He believes images are a good way to provide information.

27 What frightening experience did Ed have recently?

A He went diving in dangerous seas.

B He lost one of his safety instruments.

C He came very close to some sharks.

28 What does Ed think about his career as a marine biologist?

A He regrets not taking more risks.

B He's glad that he followed the traditional path.

C He wonders if he made the decision too early in life.

29 How do the expedition members avoid homesickness?

A by having regular contact with friends and family

B by planning group activities for quiet times

C by keeping themselves occupied

30 Ed says that he is happiest in his work when

A he spends time in the deepest areas of the sea.

B he discovers previously unknown species.

C he feels his team's reports are getting the publicity they deserve.

→ p. 122 p. 131

Test 3

READING AND USE OF ENGLISH (1 hour 15 minutes)

Part 1

For questions **1–8**, read the text below and decide which answer (**A**, **B**, **C** or **D**) best fits each gap. There is an example at the beginning (**0**).

Mark your answers **on the separate answer sheet**.

Example:

0 **A** wanting **B** asking **C** seeking **D** demanding

0	A	B	C	D
	o	●	o	o

Feedback forms

Often when we buy something or use a service, we are given a form **(0)** .... how satisfied we are with the product or the service. Many people feel that **(1)** .... such forms is a waste of time; they think that companies probably take no notice of what people put on the forms. This may be the **(2)** .... with some companies but with most nothing could be further from the **(3)** .... Surveys are carefully analysed so that problems can be **(4)** .... In fact, improvements made by companies often **(5)** .... because of what customers have written on these forms.

If you are given a form to complete, companies want you to do so in as much **(6)** .... as possible. They obviously like to receive **(7)** .... on their products but they also want customers to **(8)** .... any problems that they have found. If customers do not do this, companies may remain unaware of problems and, consequently, no improvements can be made.

1	**A**	putting down	**B**	writing up	**C**	filling in	**D**	drawing out
2	**A**	case	**B**	position	**C**	condition	**D**	state
3	**A**	experience	**B**	fact	**C**	truth	**D**	practice
4	**A**	shown	**B**	distinguished	**C**	identified	**D**	marked
5	**A**	carry out	**B**	come about	**C**	take off	**D**	open up
6	**A**	detail	**B**	evidence	**C**	point	**D**	information
7	**A**	approval	**B**	tributes	**C**	admiration	**D**	compliments
8	**A**	refer	**B**	mention	**C**	notify	**D**	advise

→ p. 133

Part 2

For questions **9–16**, read the text below and think of the word which best fits each gap. Use only **one** word in each gap. There is an example at the beginning (**0**).

Write your answers **IN CAPITAL LETTERS on the separate answer sheet.**

Example: | **0** | S | I | N | C | E |

Outdoor swimming

Ever **(0)** .... I was a young girl, I have been an enthusiastic outdoor swimmer. My favourite place to swim is the lido near my home in London – a giant pool with reflections in the sun like jewels. Being unheated, **(9)** .... can be uninviting to those **(10)** .... prefer warmer water, but that also means fewer crowds.

The swims I prefer are the ones on my own when I have the pool all to **(11)** .... Then, I slip into the water and feel it surround me. I swim up and down the pool, thinking of nothing but counting strokes between breaths: 'One, two, three, four – breathe.' Whole hours can slowly drift **(12)** .... , as my arms stretch out in **(13)** .... of me. I concentrate **(14)** .... the noise the bubbles make as I exhale under water. **(15)** .... there may be other swimmers around, I still feel alone and at peace, a sensation I don't get **(16)** .... else I know.

 → p. 133

Part 3

For questions **17–24**, read the text below. Use the word given in capitals at the end of some of the lines to form a word that fits in the gap **in the same line**. There is an example at the beginning (**0**).

Write your answers **IN CAPITAL LETTERS on the separate answer sheet.**

Example: | 0 | C | O | N | S | T | R | U | C | T | I | O | N |

The leaning tower of Pisa, Italy

In 1173, **(0)** .... work began on what was to become the **CONSTRUCT**
'Leaning Tower of Pisa'. It was, though, never the **(17)** .... of the **INTEND**
builders that the tower should lean.

Pisa was a prosperous city and expensive marble was used to build
the tower. After five years, it became **(18)** .... that the tower was **EVIDENCE**
leaning because the soft soil was incapable of fully supporting
the **(19)** .... of the marble. Work was halted for almost a **WEIGH**
hundred years because of a series of wars. However, this long
pause in the building work was **(20)** .... for the tower as it gave **FORTUNE**
the **(21)** .... time to settle. If work had continued, the tower would **FOUND**
almost certainly have collapsed.

There were later attempts to **(22)** .... the tower, but these were **STRAIGHT**
not always popular with the local inhabitants because the tower had
become a tourist attraction.

In 2008, following major **(23)** .... work on the tower, engineers **RESTORE**
(24) .... announced that the tower would remain stable for at **CONFIDENCE**
least another two hundred years.

→ p. 133

Part 4

For questions **25–30**, complete the second sentence so that it has a similar meaning to the first sentence, using the word given. **Do not change the word given**. You must use between **two** and **five** words, including the word given. Here is an example (**0**).

Example:

0 A very friendly taxi driver drove us into town.

DRIVEN

We .... a very friendly taxi driver.

The gap can be filled by the words 'were driven into town by', so you write:

Example:	**0**	*WERE DRIVEN INTO TOWN BY*

Write **only** the missing words **IN CAPITAL LETTERS on the separate answer sheet**.

---

25 My sister said to me, 'Please ring me tomorrow morning.'

GIVE

My sister asked me .... tomorrow morning.

26 Richard invited Julie to the party because he didn't want to risk offending her.

MIGHT

Richard felt Julie .... he didn't ask her to the party.

27 They let me watch television only after I had finished my homework.

ALLOWED

I .... watch television until I had finished my homework.

28 The two girls succeeded in winning the quiz by themselves.

MANAGED

In the quiz, the two girls .... own.

29 I'm sorry that I didn't spend longer with my aunt when I called on her last week.

TIME

I would like to have .... with my aunt when I called on her last week.

30 The number of students at the college is going to rise next year.

INCREASE

There .... the number of students at the college next year.

→ p. 133

Part 5

You are going to read a magazine article about a voiceover artist. For questions **31–36**, choose the answer (**A**, **B**, **C** or **D**) which you think fits best according to the text.

Mark your answers **on the separate answer sheet**.

Shirley Ford, voiceover artist

Clive Gartside meets the voiceover artist Shirley Ford, whose voice is familiar from advertisements, cartoons and other recordings.

During our first, hour-long conversation, Shirley Ford speaks to me in the voice of a cheeky 8-year-old boy, the boy's tired mother, an amusing elderly Scottish woman and a very fast-talking alien. Her voices – I struggled to keep count of them all – are recognisable to viewers of children's TV and cartoons, and to people who have seen computerised employee programmes about health and safety. 'I've just done a voiceover about back injuries,' she says, 'so I had to learn quickly how to pronounce loads of medical terms.'

Shirley talks about what it takes to do voiceovers. 'Lots of actors, some very highly regarded, reckon they can do funny voices and, actually, many of them probably can,' she says. 'There's more to it than that, though. You have to bring the script to life for an audience who can't see you. You wouldn't believe how many household names are desperate to do voiceover work. Thinking of the publicity, producers will invite them to auditions, but often they don't get offered parts because they're too used to acting with their whole bodies.'

After school, Shirley enrolled on a drama course with a standard acting career in mind. During the course, she had some occasional work singing jingles for TV adverts. 'One day,' she says, 'the man who ran the recording studio suggested I try out for the part of a rabbit in the soundtrack for a cartoon. It seemed ridiculous – I hadn't studied drama to play rabbits – but I tried it for a laugh and, amazingly, ended up getting a major part.' Shirley realised she could do voices and that voiceover work might be the way to go.

Adult female actors are frequently asked to provide the voices for small boys and girls. Their voices are lighter than those of male actors, and in the recruitment of child performers there are complex procedures and endless forms to deal with, which production companies on tight schedules would rather avoid. Shirley has learnt to create the right sounds from the back of her throat, and to avoid always sounding like the same child, she collects new voices as she watches children's TV.

Cartoons are the highlight of a job that includes a whole range of things from educational videos to vacuum cleaner adverts. 'Those are hard because you have to sound enthusiastic about something you care nothing about, but my years in this profession help,' she says. 'They've taught me that the trick is to smile while you're talking – that makes your voice sound bright and cheery. When I've got some days doing animation work, it feels like a holiday; the interaction with other actors makes a huge difference.'

The competition for work is fierce, and a good showreel – a recording demonstrating what the artist can do – is essential. 'It's definitely worth investing in a strong showreel,' Shirley says. 'There are agencies which specialise in helping voiceover artists put them together.' She claims to have got where she is – near the top of her profession – through doggedness as much as natural ability. 'Whether it's making your showreel and taking it round all the film and TV companies, advertising agencies and recording studios, or simply practising your voices, it's all about setting goals and refusing to give up.'

For anyone considering a career doing voiceovers, Shirley recommends attending 'specialist workshops – they cover all types of voiceover'. She also believes a passion for human sound is fundamental, describing herself as obsessed with voices and, in a sense, becoming the characters she is performing. 'If I've been in the studio doing a particular kind of American voice, for example, it can take control of me and I'll be speaking like that for hours, perhaps even days afterwards,' she says. 'My children have grown up used to their mum talking in completely different voices.'

31 What first impressed the writer about Shirley Ford?

A the number of her voices that seemed familiar to him
B the speed with which she could master new voices
C the ability she had to make different voices sound funny
D the wide range of voices she could produce

32 In the second paragraph, what does Shirley say about voiceover work?

A Many actors fail to take it seriously enough.
B It rarely suits actors with a background in comedy.
C It requires skills that well-known actors sometimes lack.
D Producers tend to be reluctant to consider famous actors for it.

33 What can be a problem with children doing voiceover work?

A Their voices often seem strange alongside adult voices.
B They tend to sound very similar to each other.
C Hiring them involves completing a lot of paperwork.
D It takes a long time to train them.

34 What do we learn about Shirley from the fifth paragraph?

A She understands that some jobs are more interesting than they might seem.
B She knows how to hide her lack of interest in certain kinds of work.
C She feels free to spend more time on projects that she enjoys.
D She no longer feels bad about promoting certain products.

35 The writer uses the word 'doggedness' in line 61 to refer to Shirley's

A determination to succeed.
B success in her career.
C willingness to accept support.
D knowledge of her field of work.

36 The writer's purpose in the final paragraph is to show

A how badly Shirley's career affects her family life.
B how much Shirley enjoys doing certain accents.
C how exceptionally talented Shirley is.
D how involved Shirley can get in her work.

→ p. 133

Part 6

You are going to read an article about the book *Guinness World Records*. Six sentences have been removed from the article. Choose from the sentences **A–G** the one which fits each gap (**37–42**). There is one extra sentence which you do not need to use.

Mark your answers **on the separate answer sheet.**

How to break a Guinness World Record

Who doesn't want to be the best in the world?

Why are we so fascinated by breaking records? For record holders, it is official confirmation that you can do something better than anyone else in the world, even if it is just eating a lemon quickly. People like setting goals, pushing themselves – especially if they get to see their name in print at the end of it.

Although humans have been competing and showing off for thousands of years, the official arbiter of human achievement, *Guinness World Records*, is still young. It began only 64 years ago when Sir Hugh Beaver, head of the Guinness company, got into an argument while away on a hunting trip about the fastest game bird in Europe: was it the grouse, the duck or the plover? **37** ____ And so the idea for a book of records was born, a definitive list of the world's superlatives.

It's amazing how many people seem to be interested in breaking a record. GWR gets about 1,000 record claims a week, of which only 5%–7% are accepted, and about 2% make it into the annual book. You may wonder what kind of person is interested in breaking records. Applications come from all over the world: most from the US, followed by India and China – two Indian men are currently battling for the 'longest hair' record. The typical would-be record-breaker is apparently a man in his mid-30s. **38** ____ Ashrita Furman from the US has the record for holding the most records (more than 200, though he has broken up to 600). Some people even make record attempts every day.

Almost anything definable, measurable and provable can become a record. **39** ____ Some, like those, are easy to attempt but difficult to beat, such as eating three cheese biscuits in the fastest time (34.78 seconds). It's easier to beat an existing record than set a new one because 'firsts' have to be approved as suitable records to attempt.

40 ____ The general notes spell out the importance of evidence – photographic, video, independent witnesses – as much as you can get. For mass-participation records, you must prove that you've counted properly.

GWR gives some general advice to newcomers: analyse the specific rules for your chosen record to spot and exploit any loopholes in them. For example, Furman smashed the world record for rolling an orange for a mile with his nose when he discovered the rules didn't stipulate colour – he chose an unripe green orange that was hard, round and fast. **41** ____ It isn't enough just to be able to do something unusual, such as lick your elbow. You need to have the skill to be able to lick your elbow as many times as possible in one hour – something that can then be attempted and broken by someone else.

Records will be dismissed if they are considered stupid, dangerous or illegal, or if there isn't enough evidence: an organist's playing marathon was rejected because it was only witnessed by her parents. **42** ____ Finally, don't cheat! One man, who broke the record for balancing the most drinking glasses on his chin, had his award disallowed when he admitted to breaking the rules by using plastic cups.

A They change with the times: records involving selfies have become popular recently.

B So, remember that you are responsible for proving what you've achieved.

C The mind is constantly telling you that you can't do things.

D Without the internet, there was no easy way of checking – even the host's well-stocked library couldn't settle the matter.

E Another useful idea is to choose something you're good at already and work at that.

F There is also a core of serial record breakers.

G You should apply to GWR before making your record attempt; it will send you the overall guidelines and those specific to your record.

→ p. 133

Part 7

You are going to read a magazine article about four extreme fans. For questions **43–52**, choose from the fans (**A–D**). The fans may be chosen more than once.

Mark your answers **on the separate answer sheet**.

Which fan says

she was able to improve a difficult situation through being a fan?	**43**	
she first saw her object of interest through a misunderstanding?	**44**	
her object of interest offers the best entertainment of its type?	**45**	
she is uninterested in how popular her object of interest is?	**46**	
she was concerned by what other people might think of her?	**47**	
she was encouraged to try and achieve something by being a fan?	**48**	
the object of her interest has become a part of her identity?	**49**	
she had a low expectation of something at first?	**50**	
she recognises that keeping her obsession going is a luxury?	**51**	
she was made to take an interest in something that later became her passion?	**52**	

 → p. 133

Superfans

Four women talk about the objects of their passion and dedication.

A Katie on the *Harry Potter* books

One day when I was 11, my younger sister, who was a big fan of the *Harry Potter* books, thrust the first book in the series into my hand and forced me to read it. By the next morning, I'd finished it and taken all her other *Harry Potter* books, too! I loved the fact that it was about an average child doing something extraordinary. Hermione, the clever friend of the main character, Harry, became my hero. I didn't like reading before, but because of her I wanted to be top of my class at school. The books helped me in other ways. My sister and I used to fight all the time but *Harry Potter* brought us together, gave us something in common. We even travelled to the UK so we could visit all the locations that were used for the *Harry Potter* films.

B Sally on the musical *Les Misérables*

I didn't see *Les Misérables* when it opened, thinking it didn't sound like anything special, despite all the positive reviews. When I finally went, I was amazed: it was so different from other musicals. I've been over 1,000 times now, spending more than £50,000. Because it's live theatre, every night is different. You have to keep going back to get everything out of it. I do go to other musicals but it's a risk: you may be wasting your money. When you go to *Les Misérables*, you're sure to have a good time. When I'm at the theatre, I often hear audience members saying things like: 'Oh, this is my fourth time!' I just think: 'OK, keep going!' Some people think I'm mad, but that's what I think of people who sit on cold riverbanks fishing all day.

C Cami on the opera star, Andrea Bocelli

When my husband and I started going to the opera singer Andrea Bocelli's concerts all over the world, I worried that everyone would regard us as crazy. But we made so many friends, and it was all so rewarding, that we just thought: 'Who cares?' Like many fans, I first heard him on TV. There was this programme called *A Night in Tuscany*, which I initially thought would be a travel show. There was something so touching about his voice. We've seen him 60 times now. You'd think we would be getting tired of it all, but you see something new in each show. And we've made wonderful friends. Once, we were having dinner with fans from Japan, South Africa and Europe. The only thing linking us was Andrea. It is expensive, building entire vacations around his tours, but this is our only indulgence so we don't worry about it.

D Jane on the pop singer, Madonna

My friends say I'm the most positive person they know and being a Madonna fan is part of that. I remember precisely when I first saw her on a TV music show. I was only watching because I was bored. Then Madonna appeared on screen and I was transfixed by this young woman with such amazing energy. Slowly the Madonna posters started going up in my room. Soon, I was travelling to concerts around the world. I couldn't care less if she is no longer regarded as the coolest star – being a Madonna fan is important to how I see myself – my sense of self. I've now been to over 90 performances. A Madonna show is like a modern circus: spectacular lights, costumes and dancers. Even without her, it would be fantastic. Madonna isn't my only obsession, but she's the one that provides the most fun. I've met some of my best friends through Madonna.

WRITING (1 hour 20 minutes)

Part 1

You **must** answer this question. Write your answer in **140–190** words in an appropriate style on the separate answer sheet.

---

1 In your English class you have been talking about advertising. Now, your English teacher has asked you to write an essay.

Write your essay using **all** the notes and giving reasons for your point of view.

'Advertisements which are aimed at children should not be allowed.'

What do you think?

Notes

Write about:

1. They can be entertaining and fun.

2. They encourage unnecessary spending.

3. .... (your own idea)

→ p. 105

Part 2

Write an answer to **one** of the questions **2–4** in this part. Write your answer in **140–190** words in an appropriate style on the separate answer sheet. Put the question number in the box at the top of the answer sheet.

---

2 You have received this email from your Canadian friend, Nick.

> **Subject:** What to study
>
> I have to decide what subject to study at university next year. I'm good at English Literature, Engineering and History, and I like them all equally. But I just can't make up my mind which one to choose.
>
> What do you think I should do?
>
> Best wishes
>
> Nick

Write your **email**.

3 You see this notice on a website.

> **Articles wanted**
>
> **Relaxation**
>
> What does relaxation mean to you and how do you usually relax?
> Why is it important for people to relax?
>
> The best articles will be published on our website.

Write your **article**.

4 You have seen this notice in a magazine.

> **Reviews wanted**
>
> **Restaurants for special occasions**
>
> We are looking for reviews of restaurants which are good places to celebrate special occasions.
>
> In your review you should:
>
> - describe the restaurant and the food it serves
> - say what special occasions you would recommend the restaurant for.
>
> The best reviews will be published next month.

Write your **review**.

→ p. 106

LISTENING (approximately 40 minutes)

Listening test audio

Part 1

You will hear people talking in eight different situations.
For questions **1–8**, choose the best answer (**A**, **B** or **C**).

---

1 You hear a man talking to a friend about a bicycle shop.

What is he doing?

A recommending the shop to her

B explaining how she can get to the shop

C suggesting she should have her bike repaired

2 You hear a TV producer talking about reality programmes on TV.

What is the main point she makes about popular reality shows?

A The production standards are very high.

B They deserve the praise they get.

C Their popularity is short-lived.

3 You hear two writers talking about writing dialogue.

What do they agree about?

A Most writers reproduce dialogue they have overheard.

B Less experienced writers should work hard to improve their dialogue.

C Good writers have a natural ability to write dialogue.

4 You hear a woman telling a friend about a long train journey she's been on.

Why did the woman enjoy it?

A She had some interesting conversations.

B She saw some beautiful scenery.

C She had a comfortable seat.

5 You hear a man telling a friend about a holiday he's recently been on.

He wishes that he'd

A taken more photographs.

B booked his accommodation online.

C got hold of a good guidebook.

6 You hear a woman talking on the radio about the arts.

What is she talking about?

A a book she knows well

B a TV programme she enjoyed watching

C a film she has seen many times

7 You hear two students discussing their college.

What do they both like about it?

A the attitude of the teachers

B the state of the decoration

C the quality of the sports facilities

8 You hear a child psychologist talking about the impact of noise on very young children.

In his view, it is the parents' responsibility to

A speak more clearly when the environment is noisy.

B appreciate the particular problems noise causes.

C ensure the amount of noise is kept constant.

→ p. 134 p. 135

Part 2

You will hear a woman called Jane Hughes talking about total solar eclipses, which happen when the Moon comes between the Sun and the Earth and blocks out the light from the Sun. For questions **9–18**, complete the sentences with a word or short phrase.

Listening test audio

Total solar eclipses

Jane says she was encouraged to go and see a total solar eclipse by an interesting

(9) .... she saw.

Jane hired a **(10)** .... to travel to the best location to watch her first eclipse.

The eclipse Jane saw took place during the early **(11)** ....

Jane says watching the eclipse was as exciting for her as doing a

(12) ....

Jane says the effect at the beginning and end of an eclipse resembles a

(13) ....

Jane had to go to a **(14)** .... to see her second eclipse.

A lack of **(15)** .... nearly caused Jane's boat journey to be cancelled.

Jane says she was pleased she had a **(16)** .... to hang over herself at night.

Jane's **(17)** .... about watching eclipses can be found online.

Jane is going to get a new **(18)** .... before she watches her next eclipse.

→ p. 134 p. 139

Part 3

You will hear five short extracts in which people are talking about walking to work. For questions **19–23**, choose from the list (**A–H**) how each speaker says they benefit from walking to work. Use the letters only once. There are three extra letters which you do not need to use.

Listening test audio

A I have more energy for work.

B I now appreciate the good things in my life.

C I am able to adapt my route to how I am feeling.

D I get to and from work more quickly.

E It has motivated me to have a better diet.

F I have been able to appreciate the history of the area better.

G I'm sharing an experience with others.

H I've found it a good alternative to other types of exercise.

Speaker	Answer	Question
Speaker 1		**19**
Speaker 2		**20**
Speaker 3		**21**
Speaker 4		**22**
Speaker 5		**23**

→ p. 134 p. 141

Part 4

Listening test audio

You will hear an interview with a woman called Sarah Featherstone, who runs a website called Coffee Lovers. For questions **24–30**, choose the best answer (**A**, **B** or **C**).

---

24 Sarah says she started her website to try to

A help a particular type of coffee shop.

B inform tourists with a limited budget.

C change the attitude of certain big companies.

25 What does Sarah say about changes to the website?

A Reviews from users are the main feature.

B Interested clients have to apply to be included.

C The basic design layout has been reorganised.

26 The most likely reason for excluding a coffee shop from the website is

A an unattractive building.

B poor customer service.

C the taste of the product.

27 What does Sarah praise the Old Mill House coffee shop for?

A the style of their notices to customers

B the attractive interior

C the entertainment they provide

28 What does Sarah think about the food served in the Pink Peacock?

A It's the best takeaway food in the neighbourhood.

B It's suitable for those with special dietary needs.

C It's good value for money.

29 When setting up her own business, Sarah was very aware of the need

A to try out a completely new field.

B to avoid taking financial risks.

C not to repeat previous mistakes.

30 When asked about plans for her website, Sarah says her immediate priority is

A to introduce a star system.

B to experiment with an international section.

C to develop a new app.

→ p. 134 p. 143

Test 4

READING AND USE OF ENGLISH (1 hour 15 minutes)

Part 1

For questions **1–8**, read the text below and decide which answer (**A**, **B**, **C** or **D**) best fits each gap. There is an example at the beginning (**0**).

Mark your answers **on the separate answer sheet.**

Example:

0 **A** strong **B** deep **C** thorough **D** heavy

0	A	B	C	D
	o	●	o	o

Chimpanzee beds

One morning, Koichiro Zamma, a zoologist at Japan's Kyoto University, awoke from a **(0)** .... sleep in the treetops of an African forest. For years, he had been **(1)** .... for the perfect night's sleep. His **(2)** .... sleep that night had not involved special mattresses or pillows. It had been on a construction of leaves, **(3)** .... together by twigs, and built by chimpanzees.

Zamma noticed that chimpanzees' beds are built to **(4)** .... the exact shape of their bodies. They're built high up in trees, and sway gently with the movement of the branches, which aids sleep. He realised they could serve as a useful **(5)** .... for the perfect human bed.

Zamma has now designed a bed based on the principles of the chimpanzee bed. The mattress **(6)** .... a depression in the centre to imitate the natural dip in the chimpanzee bed. This is supported by a frame which **(7)** .... the bed to gently move. Some enthusiasts **(8)** .... the bed has transformed their sleeping habits.

	A		B		C		D	
1	**A**	inquiring	**B**	wanting	**C**	searching	**D**	attempting
2	**A**	restoring	**B**	refreshing	**C**	relieving	**D**	renewing
3	**A**	gripped	**B**	grasped	**C**	pushed	**D**	held
4	**A**	coincide	**B**	fit	**C**	follow	**D**	correspond
5	**A**	model	**B**	standard	**C**	imitation	**D**	example
6	**A**	promotes	**B**	demonstrates	**C**	consists	**D**	features
7	**A**	admits	**B**	allows	**C**	encourages	**D**	provides
8	**A**	respond	**B**	promote	**C**	claim	**D**	recommend

→ p. 145

Part 2

For questions **9–16**, read the text below and think of the word which best fits each gap. Use only **one** word in each gap. There is an example at the beginning (**0**).

Write your answers **IN CAPITAL LETTERS on the separate answer sheet.**

Example: | 0 | | O | F |

New Year's resolutions

At the start **(0)** .... each new year, people in some countries make resolutions for the future. These resolutions are intentions that people aim to fulfil in the hope of changing their lives **(9)** .... the better. Resolutions range from giving **(10)** .... a bad habit such as smoking **(11)** .... beginning a new activity, for example learning to play a musical instrument.

Unfortunately, many people find keeping their resolutions very difficult and, a month **(12)** .... so later, abandon them. This is often a result of having set a totally unrealistic goal for themselves.

The people who are most successful in keeping their resolutions **(13)** .... usually those who make sure that their goals are fairly small and straightforward. They have a clear idea of precisely **(14)** .... they plan to do to reach their goal. Often they find **(15)** .... helpful if they have friends who have made the same resolution because they are then able to support one **(16)** .... in remaining committed and focused.

 → p. 145

Part 3

For questions **17–24**, read the text below. Use the word given in capitals at the end of some of the lines to form a word that fits in the gap **in the same line**. There is an example at the beginning (**0**).

Write your answers **IN CAPITAL LETTERS on the separate answer sheet.**

Example: | 0 | F A M O U S |

Alfred Hitchcock

One of the most **(0)** .... filmmakers of the twentieth century was	**FAME**
Alfred Hitchcock. He was born in England and had considerable	
(17) .... making films there before he decided to move to the	**SUCCEED**
United States to work in Hollywood.	
Hitchcock is best remembered for his **(18)** .... thrillers, such as	**PSYCHOLOGY**
Psycho. He had great skill in building up **(19)** .... , which made his	**TENSE**
films extremely **(20)** .... for audiences.	**FRIGHTEN**
Hitchcock liked to make a brief **(21)** .... in most of his films – at	**APPEAR**
times that were in no way essential to the plot. When he realised	
audiences were waiting eagerly for him to appear, he started to make	
sure that these moments occurred early in the films to avoid being a	
(22) .... from the plot.	**DISTRACT**
It was sometimes said that Hitchcock had no great liking for actors.	
This was something of an **(23)** .... , but there is certainly some	**EXAGGERATE**
(24) .... in it as he did not enjoy working with actors who disagreed	**TRUE**
with the way he interpreted their parts.	

→ p. 145

Part 4

For questions **25–30**, complete the second sentence so that it has a similar meaning to the first sentence, using the word given. **Do not change the word given**. You must use between **two** and **five** words, including the word given. Here is an example (**0**).

Example:

0 A very friendly taxi driver drove us into town.

DRIVEN

We .... a very friendly taxi driver.

The gap can be filled by the words 'were driven into town by', so you write:

Example:	**0**	*WERE DRIVEN INTO TOWN BY*

Write **only** the missing words **IN CAPITAL LETTERS on the separate answer sheet.**

---

25 My mother once worked for an engineering company.

EMPLOYED

My mother used .... an engineering company.

26 It rained without stopping last Friday.

NEVER

It .... last Friday.

27 I'm having difficulty understanding the instructions on my new camera.

DIFFICULT

I am finding .... the instructions on my new camera.

28 People are spending more money on leisure activities than in the past.

INCREASE

There has been .... the amount of money people are spending on leisure activities.

29 The city needs to have a far better transport system.

NEED

The city is .... a far better transport system.

30 You should be more careful with your handwriting.

ATTENTION

You ought .... your handwriting.

→ p. 145

Part 5

You are going to read a magazine article about being a cartoonist. For questions **31–36**, choose the answer (**A**, **B**, **C** or **D**) which you think fits best according to the text.

Mark your answers **on the separate answer sheet**.

So you want to be a cartoonist?

People are always asking me how I became a cartoonist. This is understandable – cartooning is one of those jobs you dream about as a little kid, like being a race car driver. But most people eventually throw these childish daydreams away and consider more realistic professions, like becoming a tax lawyer or a manufacturer of auto parts. The idea that you can support yourself financially at all, let alone maintain an adequate lifestyle, by sketching the sort of doodles commonly found in the margins of high school notebooks is, when you think about it,
line 13 silly. Yet some people do exactly that.

As for me, after having a fairly typical cartoonist's childhood (obsessive love of comic strips, contributions to school publications, being known throughout school as 'the kid who draws'), I happened to study graphic design in college and then, after graduating, went around different companies with a collection of illustrations. I was lucky to find someone at a newspaper who told me they were looking for political cartoons on local issues. I drew up a few ideas and they bought them; in a few months, I was selling enough to support myself.

You actually don't need much to become a cartoonist. You don't need a university degree, you don't need much money, you don't even really need to know how to draw. You just need your brain, your hand and something that makes a mark. But of course, if it really was that easy, there would be as many cartoonists as there are, say, teachers. The technical barriers to being a cartoonist are low, but it's a tough job nevertheless. No one should attempt to enter the profession unless they feel that doing anything else would be impossible. After all, it's so much easier to get a regular job that pays the rent and leaves at least a little time for the family, home repairs and hobbies.

The more things you know how to do well, the more chance you have of making a living with your art. I've done political cartoons, comic strips and comic books. I've also been a writer, a caricaturist and occasionally a designer. I don't turn down anything – that's because you can learn an awful lot even from work you don't particularly want to do. It also doesn't hurt to be intelligent, well-read and curious about everything around you.

But what about the business side of being a cartoonist? There was a time when a significant number of cartoonists could find regular jobs doing cartoons for several different newspapers and magazines. But those days, if they aren't gone, are rapidly passing. For almost everyone today, cartooning is an entrepreneurial activity – that means you're not just going to have to produce the work, you're going to have to sell it. The more comfortable you are with what that involves, the better you'll do. Time and time again, I've seen cartoonists with average creative abilities and excellent business skills do far better than those who were artistic geniuses but nothing else.

It amazes me how often I meet people who have never sold a cartoon in their life and yet are terrified someone will steal their ideas. Some of these people are so worried that they refuse to let others even look at their work! Legally, all you need to do to protect your stuff is draw a little 'c' for 'copyright' somewhere, put a circle around the letter, then write your name and the date next to it. But let's face it – it's far more realistic that no one will be interested in your work. If, by some chance, someone steals a cartoon and it goes viral on the internet and everybody starts emailing it to their friends, it's not a disaster – it can be an extremely lucky break, publicity-wise!

31 In the first paragraph, what point does the writer make about being a cartoonist?

A It is not seen as a very practical career option.
B People prefer doing jobs that have a higher status.
C People are surprised at how little money cartoonists get.
D Not enough children are being encouraged to become one.

32 What does 'that' in line 13 refer to?

A thinking about things too much
B supporting yourself financially
C sketching doodles in school notebooks
D considering a different profession

33 The writer mentions teachers to make the point that

A professional cartoonists need time to develop their skills.
B professional cartoonists need to have a passion for their work.
C it is harder to become a professional cartoonist than it might seem.
D many professional cartoonists complain of not having much free time.

34 In the fourth paragraph, the writer suggests professional cartoonists

A learn from other types of artists.
B do thorough research for jobs.
C work on different projects at the same time.
D accept even unappealing jobs.

35 What does the writer say about dealing with the business side of being a cartoonist?

A It can be distracting.
B It is unavoidable.
C It is difficult to do well.
D It can be exhausting.

36 What does the writer say about the theft of ideas from cartoonists?

A It is highly unlikely to happen.
B People are more aware of it now.
C The law does not prevent it happening.
D The internet has made it easier to do.

→ p. 145

Part 6

You are going to read an article from a magazine about an unusual hobby. Six sentences have been removed from the article. Choose from the sentences **A–G** the one which fits each gap (**37–42**). There is one extra sentence which you do not need to use.

Mark your answers **on the separate answer sheet.**

Messages in bottles

I was 22 and on a family holiday in the Caribbean Turks and Caicos Islands when it first happened. As we strode along the beach, I saw a glint of blue glass on the shoreline. I realised it was a large bottle – and that there was something inside it. I was so excited!

I'd always dreamed of finding a message in a bottle and my hands were shaking as I uncorked it. It turned out the bottle had been dropped eight months previously by a couple on board a cruise from the Portuguese island of Madeira. **37** ______ This bottle had managed to survive its journey all the way across the Atlantic and I'd found it.

I emailed the senders as soon as I got back to the hotel. They were happy to know someone had got their message, but perhaps disappointed that it had been found so soon after they'd dropped it overboard. For me, however, it was a profound experience. **38** ______ My family and I had always beach-combed for shells on vacation, and when you learn how to look properly, you start finding loads. I figured that I could do the same with messages in bottles.

Since that holiday, eight years ago, I've found more than 80 messages in bottles, mostly on the Turks and Caicos Islands, which oceanographer Curtis Ebbesmeyer calls 'a magnet for floating objects'. Bottles have been washing up on the islands since at least the 1800s; the Turks and Caicos National Museum features a large collection. I've picked up bottles from senders in North America, Europe and Asia. **39** ______ I've also found artwork, business cards, dollar bills ... even a crumbling piece of wedding cake.

I try to make contact with the senders if I can. **40** ______ I travelled to Düsseldorf last summer to meet Sabine Roy, a German travel agent whose message I found back in 2011. Sabine's message had deteriorated badly by the time I'd found it; all I could make out was a cruise ship letterhead, her name and 'Düsseldorf'. I tried tracing her for four years before I thought of posting a message on social media. Within a day, I had tracked her down.

It's a very strange experience when I meet a sender. We've been brought together entirely by chance and there are no guarantees we'll have anything in common. **41** ______ People who send messages in bottles tend to be adventurous types and are often as excited to meet up as I am.

A lot of people forget they've sent these messages and when you present them with these pieces of their past, it's almost like time travel. **42** ______ When I called the phone number supplied, in Baltimore, USA, I spoke to an elderly woman. She told me her young son must have sent the bottle while on a boat trip with his dad in the 1990s. It's discoveries like these that keep me interested in hunting for bottles.

A It's not just messages inside either.

B So you might think these encounters could be awkward – although that hasn't been my experience so far.

C One of the oldest messages I found was from a soft drinks bottle from the 1970s.

D It wasn't a treasure map or a cry for help from someone stranded on a deserted island, but to me, it was a miracle.

E Sometimes it's funny, as was the case with a note I found from a sender who claimed to have been 'taken prisoner by a grumpy old monster'.

F It sparked a sort of obsession and I started spending every spare cent and every spare moment looking for more bottles.

G The internet has made that easier than it would have been in the past and I often get help through my blog and web page.

→ p. 145

Part 7

You are going to read a magazine article about working as a sports psychologist. For questions **43–52**, choose from the sections (**A–E**). The sections may be chosen more than once.

Mark your answers **on the separate answer sheet**.

In which section are the following mentioned?

the need to appreciate the process of competing	**43**	
the need for patience to achieve success	**44**	
an increased level of curiosity about how psychology can help in sport	**45**	
the apparent difficulty of giving instruction in the use of mental strategies	**46**	
understanding from experience what sports professionals require	**47**	
how recent research findings can aid sportspeople	**48**	
sportspeople's feelings having a negative effect on them	**49**	
greater awareness of what sports psychologists do these days	**50**	
the importance for sportspeople of maintaining focus	**51**	
a tendency to see successful people as having no weaknesses	**52**	

 → p. 145

What does a sports psychologist do?

Jeremy Snape explains

A I set up my company Sporting Edge a decade ago to share the practical tools which promote success in sport. I specialise in the mental side of high performance. The role of the sports psychologist is more widely accepted than it was when I set up my company. Nowadays, when people reach the very top of their professions, we often hear that it was their mental game that led to their success. With so many world champions in sport speaking positively about their mental training now, it has created a new drive for sportspeople to find out what they could achieve with it. There used to be more mistrust of the concept of sports psychology. I think this is because our society celebrates people who are presented as being perfect, so it's a contradiction for these people to express any doubts or have any flaws. Thankfully, it's now seen as a positive thing, not a failing, to deal with imperfections in the mental game as readily as we do in the physical one.

B Part of my role involves working with players and coaches to focus on the things that create the conditions for success. I teach them not to be overly influenced by the emotions that can impact badly on performance. When they can do this, they are able to create a clearer and more logical plan for success. We all want instant success, but if you take the time to develop quality long-term plans and not just concentrate on thorough preparation in the short term, you have a chance of reaching your potential. As a former international sportsman myself, I know very well the importance of this.

C The latest scientific discoveries can help athletes' state of mind. For example, developments in functional MRI scanning and neuroscience show us that talking to ourselves isn't meaningless, as is commonly thought – it actually creates structures in the brain which, if reinforced repeatedly, can influence our actions and thus our success or failure. We therefore have a responsibility to ensure that our thinking habits are as healthy as possible. Learning routines to develop concentration is crucial. Athletes need to forget about everything else and keep their minds on their game. Mental strength is definitely something that can be trained and developed like physical strength.

D The vast majority of training within teams will be physical rather than mental, but there are mental skills running through every physical session – decision-making, understanding team behaviour, confidence, focus, and so on. When coaches place an emphasis on these, it can really make a difference. The problem is that they seem harder to coach and that's where a sports psychologist can help. We can help coaches find new ways of reinforcing psychological skills. We can help them develop the way they deliver instructions, get feedback after skills sessions or facilitate team discussions in meetings. Forward-thinking coaches know that this is the way to engage and motivate players.

E Elite performers are often driven by a fear of failure and feel a strong sense of relief after they succeed. This is because so much of people's identity is made up of what we do for a job rather than who we really are. This means we are desperate to be considered a success and not to let anyone down. If we tried to enjoy the struggle more, rather than just the end result, we would see that this is actually where the fun is. Professional sport is defined by results, though, so we have to accept that our careers will be remembered for those moments when we win something.

WRITING (1 hour 20 minutes)

Part 1

You **must** answer this question. Write your answer in **140–190** words in an appropriate style on the separate answer sheet.

---

1 In your English class you have been talking about family life. Now, your English teacher has asked you to write an essay.

Write your essay using **all** the notes and giving reasons for your point of view.

Is it better to be part of a large family or a small family?

Notes

Write about:

1. cost

2. learning from others

3. .... (your own idea)

→ p. 107

Part 2

Write an answer to **one** of the questions **2–4** in this part. Write your answer in **140–190** words in an appropriate style on the separate answer sheet. Put the question number in the box at the top of the answer sheet.

---

2 You recently saw this notice in a magazine.

> **Reviews wanted**
>
> **Useful books**
>
> Write us a review of a useful book which you have read.
>
> In your review describe what the book is about, explain how it was useful to you and say why you would recommend it to others.

Write your **review**.

3 You see this notice in a travel magazine.

> **Wanted – people to join Arctic expedition**
>
> Our organization is researching life in the Arctic. We are looking for people to join our two-month expedition next year. You should be able to work in a team, have skills that are useful in an Arctic environment and have a good level of English.
>
> Write to expedition organizer, Roger Beard, explaining why you would be suitable to join our expedition.

Write your **letter of application**.

4 You see this announcement on an English-language website.

> Articles wanted
>
> **An important decision**
>
> Write us an article about an important decision you've made. In your article you should say what you had to decide, explain how easy or difficult it was to make the decision, and say what effect it had on your life.

Write your **article**.

→ p. 108

LISTENING (approximately 40 minutes)

Listening test audio

Part 1

You will hear people talking in eight different situations. For questions **1–8**, choose the best answer (**A**, **B** or **C**).

---

1 You hear an actress talking about her new part in a play.

Why did she choose to accept it?

A She wanted to work with the main male actor.

B She was attracted by the strong female role.

C She wanted a change from her TV work.

2 You hear two friends talking about a restaurant.

What do they agree about it?

A The service could be improved.

B The food looked unappealing.

C The interior was badly designed.

3 You hear two students talking about a visit to a museum.

What does the man say about their guide?

A He knew a lot about the exhibits.

B He gave clear answers to questions.

C He made a difficult subject interesting.

4 You hear a talk given by a child psychologist.

The purpose of her talk is to

A warn of the potential dangers of outdoor play.

B highlight the findings of some recent health research.

C persuade people to give their children more freedom.

5 You hear part of a radio phone-in discussion about a proposal to redevelop one part of a city.

Why is the man calling the programme?

A to express concern about how the project may affect local residents

B to question the motivation behind the plan

C to point out the likely environmental impact of any changes

6 You hear two people talking on the radio about an exhibition of work by a wildlife photographer.

What do they both say about the photos?

A The lack of variety was disappointing.

B The technique used in them was unusual.

C The photographer's aims were unclear.

7 You hear a man telling a colleague about a workshop he will attend.

What does the man have to do before the workshop?

A listen to some online material

B read some written information

C think of some questions to bring up

8 You hear two friends talking about the football team they support.

How does the man feel about the manager of the team?

A concerned about his ability to motivate the players

B disappointed with the style of play he encourages

C worried about his attitude towards journalists

→ p. 146 p. 147

Part 2

You will hear a man called Victor Medway talking to some students about his job, helping to organise a music festival. For questions **9–18**, complete the sentences with a word or short phrase.

Listening test audio

Helping to organise a music festival

Victor worked as a **(9)** .... for radio programmes before becoming a festival organiser.

Victor's work as a volunteer involved **(10)** .... at a music festival.

Victor recently booked a well-known group who play **(11)** .... music for this year's music festival.

A maximum number of **(12)** .... people are allowed to attend the festival.

Victor says that criticising his festival for a lack of **(13)** .... is no longer fair.

The festival will include **(14)** .... acts as a new feature this year.

Victor attends other music festivals for the **(15)** .... they provide.

Victor welcomes the development of a **(16)** .... of festival organisers.

Victor says he's surprised that musicians' **(17)** .... are sometimes difficult to work with.

Victor has worked hard to improve his **(18)** .... skills.

 → p. 146 p. 151

Part 3

You will hear five short extracts in which people are talking about a cookery course they participated in. For questions **19–23**, choose from the list (**A–H**) what each speaker liked best about the course. Use the letters only once. There are three extra letters which you do not need to use.

Listening test audio

A watching a professional cook an unusual dish

B using modern equipment

C meeting different people

D cooking with fresh ingredients

E learning new cooking techniques

F trying other people's cooking

G mastering new recipes

H discovering how quick some dishes can be to cook

Speaker		
Speaker 1		**19**
Speaker 2		**20**
Speaker 3		**21**
Speaker 4		**22**
Speaker 5		**23**

→ p. 146 p. 153

Part 4

Listening test audio

You will hear an interview with Terry Bankcroft, whose company Get Running organises overseas marathons, talking about his work. For questions **24–30**, choose the best answer (**A**, **B** or **C**).

---

24 Terry got involved in running because he was

A keen to change his lifestyle.

B interested in starting a new hobby.

C motivated to do so by another person.

25 What does Terry say about his own running?

A It's a fundamental part of his life.

B It's less enjoyable than other sports.

C He now prefers to do shorter races.

26 Terry thinks the most challenging aspect of organising a race is

A justifying the cost of the race fee to the runners.

B dealing with people in authority overseas.

C ensuring that preparations are completed on time.

27 What is important to Terry when considering a location for a new race?

A how easily accessible it is

B how well he knows the area

C how visually appealing the landscape is

28 Terry says the volunteers who help out at his races

A are often new to running.

B get little recognition for the work they do.

C find helping at events rewarding.

29 Terry explains that the race package tours for overseas participants

A cover the cost of air travel.

B are handled exclusively by local companies.

C include local accommodation.

30 What is Terry's advice to people who are racing for the first time?

A Try to get a good position early on in the race.

B Concentrate on running your own race.

C Take great care to avoid any injuries.

→ p. 146 p. 155

Speaking tests

Test 1

Note: The visual material for Test 1 appears on pages 164–166.

Example Speaking test video

Part 1
2 minutes (3 minutes for groups of three)

Interlocutor

Good morning/afternoon/evening. My name is ………… and this is my colleague ………… .
And your names are?
Can I have your mark sheets, please?
Thank you.

- Where are you from, *(Candidate A)*?
- And you, *(Candidate B)*?

First, we'd like to know something about you.

Select one or more questions from any of the following categories, as appropriate.

Family and friends

- Who are you most like in your family? (In what ways are you similar?)
- Do you go on holiday with your family? (Why? / Why not?)
- Have you done anything interesting with your friends recently? (What did you do with them?)
- Tell me about a really good friend of yours. (Do you share the same interests?)

Your interests

- Is there a sport or hobby you enjoy doing? (What do you do?) (Why do you like it?)
- If you could learn a new skill, what would you choose to do? (Why?)
- Do you like reading? (What do you read?) (Why do you like it?)
- Have you seen a good film recently? (Tell me about it.)

Future plans

- Have you got any plans for this weekend? (What are you going to do?)
- Are you going to go on holiday this year? (Where are you going to go?)
- Is there anything you'd like to study in the future? (Why?)
- Which country would you most like to visit in the future? (Do you think you'll go there one day?) (Why? / Why not?)

Part 2
4 minutes (6 minutes for groups of three)

A Using laptops in different places

Interlocutor	In this part of the test, I'm going to give each of you two photographs. I'd like you to talk about your photographs on your own for about a minute, and also to answer a question about your partner's photographs. *(Candidate A)*, it's your turn first. Here are your photographs. They show people who are using laptops in different places. *Indicate the pictures on page 164 to the candidates.* I'd like you to compare the photographs, and say why you think the people are using laptops in these different places. All right?
Candidate A	*[1 minute.]*
Interlocutor	Thank you. *(Candidate B)*, do you often use a laptop? (Why? / Why not?)
Candidate B	*[Approximately 30 seconds.]*
Interlocutor	Thank you.

B Learning about the natural world

Interlocutor	Now, *(Candidate B)*, here are your photographs. They show people learning about the natural world in different places. *Indicate the pictures on page 165 to the candidates.* I'd like you to compare the photographs, and say why you think the people are learning about the natural world in these places. All right?
Candidate B	*[1 minute.]*
Interlocutor	Thank you. *(Candidate A)*, which place would you prefer to go to? (Why?)
Candidate A	*[Approximately 30 seconds.]*
Interlocutor	Thank you.

Part 3	4 minutes (5 minutes for groups of three)
Part 4	4 minutes (6 minutes for groups of three)

Part 3 Making plans

Interlocutor	Now, I'd like you to talk about something together for about two minutes (*3 minutes for groups of three*). Some people think that it's important to plan everything carefully. Here are some things people often make plans about and a question for you to discuss. First you have some time to look at the task. *Indicate the text on page 166 to the candidates. Allow 15 seconds.* Now, talk to each other about whether it's important to plan these things carefully.
Candidates	*[2 minutes (3 minutes for groups of three).]*
Interlocutor	Thank you. Now you have about a minute to decide which is the most important thing to plan carefully.
Candidates	*[1 minute (for pairs and groups of three).]*
Interlocutor	Thank you.

Part 4

Interlocutor Use the following questions, in order, as appropriate:

- Do you like making plans for the future? (Why? / Why not?)
- Is it important for students to make plans about the future while they're still at school? (Why? / Why not?)
- Do you think it's true that people who plan their lives carefully are more likely to lead happy lives? (Why? / Why not?)
- Do you think young children should be allowed to plan how they spend their time? (Why? / Why not?)
- Some people say that the best times in life are never planned. Do you agree? (Why? / Why not?)
- Some people say that before making a big decision we should talk to as many people as possible. Do you agree? (Why? / Why not?)

Select any of the following prompts, as appropriate:

- What do you think?
- Do you agree?
- And you?

Thank you. That is the end of the test.

Test 2

Note: The visual material for Test 2 appears on pages 167–169.

Part 1
2 minutes (3 minutes for groups of three)

Interlocutor

Good morning/afternoon/evening. My name is ………… and this is my colleague ………… .
And your names are?
Can I have your mark sheets, please?
Thank you.

- Where are you from, *(Candidate A)*?
- And you, *(Candidate B)*?

First, we'd like to know something about you.

Select one or more questions from any of the following categories, as appropriate.

Family and friends

- Who are you most like in your family? (In what ways are you similar?)
- Do you go on holiday with your family? (Why? / Why not?)
- Have you done anything interesting with your friends recently?
  (What did you do with them?)
- Tell me about a really good friend of yours. (Do you share the same interests?)

Your interests

- Is there a sport or hobby you enjoy doing? (What do you do?) (Why do you like it?)
- If you could learn a new skill, what would you choose to do? (Why?)
- Do you like reading? (What do you read?) (Why do you like it?)
- Have you seen a good film recently? (Tell me about it.)

Future plans

- Have you got any plans for this weekend? (What are you going to do?)
- Are you going to go on holiday this year? (Where are you going to go?)
- Is there anything you'd like to study in the future? (Why?)
- Which country would you most like to visit in the future?
  (Do you think you'll go there one day?) (Why? / Why not?)

Part 2

4 minutes (6 minutes for groups of three)

A Spending time in the forest

Interlocutor	In this part of the test, I'm going to give each of you two photographs. I'd like you to talk about your photographs on your own for about a minute, and also to answer a question about your partner's photographs. *(Candidate A)*, it's your turn first. Here are your photographs. They show people spending time in a forest. *Indicate the pictures on page 167 to the candidates.* I'd like you to compare the photographs, and say what you think the people are enjoying about spending time in the forest. All right?
Candidate A	*[1 minute.]*
Interlocutor	Thank you. *(Candidate B)*, do you like visiting forests? (Why? / Why not?)
Candidate B	*[Approximately 30 seconds.]*
Interlocutor	Thank you.

B Helping other people

Interlocutor	Now, *(Candidate B)*, here are your photographs. They show people who need help. *Indicate the pictures on page 168 to the candidates.* I'd like you to compare the photographs, and say why you think the people need help in these situations. All right?
Candidate B	*[1 minute.]*
Interlocutor	Thank you. *(Candidate A)*, do you / did you enjoy painting at school? (Why? / Why not?)
Candidate A	*[Approximately 30 seconds.]*
Interlocutor	Thank you.

Part 3	4 minutes (5 minutes for groups of three)
Part 4	4 minutes (6 minutes for groups of three)

Part 3 Sharing ideas online

Interlocutor	Now, I'd like you to talk about something together for about two minutes (*3 minutes for groups of three*). Some people think it's good to share ideas with other people online, for example on forums, blogs and social media sites. Here are some things they think about and a question for you to discuss. First you have some time to look at the task. *Indicate the text on page 169 to the candidates. Allow 15 seconds.* Now, talk to each other about whether it's good or bad to share ideas with other people online.
Candidates	*[2 minutes (3 minutes for groups of three).]*
Interlocutor	Thank you. Now you have about a minute to decide which is the best reason for sharing ideas with other people online.
Candidates	*[1 minute (for pairs and groups of three).]*
Interlocutor	Thank you.

Part 4

Interlocutor

Use the following questions, in order, as appropriate:

- Do you spend a lot of time talking to friends online? (Why? / Why not?)
- Do you think it's true that meeting friends face-to-face is always better than chatting online? (Why? / Why not?)
- Some people say that students can learn more online than in the classroom. What do you think? (Why?)
- Some people say we don't really need books any more because we can find all the information we need online. What do you think? (Why?)
- Do you think that performing songs online or writing things online is a good way for people to become famous? (Why? / Why not?)
- Do you think that people will spend more or less time online in the future? (Why? / Why not?)

Select any of the following prompts, as appropriate:

- What do you think?
- Do you agree?
- And you?

Thank you. That is the end of the test.

Test 3

Note: The visual material for Test 3 appears on pages 170–172.

Part 1
2 minutes (3 minutes for groups of three)

Interlocutor

Good morning/afternoon/evening. My name is .... and this is my colleague ....
And your names are?
Can I have your mark sheets, please?
Thank you.

- Where are you from, *(Candidate A)*?
- And you, *(Candidate B)*?

First, we'd like to know something about you.

Select one or more questions from any of the following categories, as appropriate.

Family and friends

- Who are you most like in your family? (In what ways are you similar?)
- Do you go on holiday with your family? (Why? / Why not?)
- Have you done anything interesting with your friends recently? (What did you do with them?)
- Tell me about a really good friend of yours. (Do you share the same interests?)

Your interests

- Is there a sport or hobby you enjoy doing? (What do you do?) (Why do you like it?)
- If you could learn a new skill, what would you choose to do? (Why?)
- Do you like reading? (What do you read?) (Why do you like it?)
- Have you seen a good film recently? (Tell me about it.)

Future plans

- Have you got any plans for this weekend? (What are you going to do?)
- Are you going to go on holiday this year? (Where are you going to go?)
- Is there anything you'd like to study in the future? (Why?)
- Which country would you most like to visit in the future? (Do you think you'll go there one day?) (Why? / Why not?)

Part 2
4 minutes (6 minutes for groups of three)

A Resting

Interlocutor	In this part of the test, I'm going to give each of you two photographs. I'd like you to talk about your photographs on your own for about a minute, and also to answer a question about your partner's photographs. *(Candidate A)*, it's your turn first. Here are your photographs. They show people resting in different places. *Indicate the pictures on page 170 to the candidates.* I'd like you to compare the photographs, and say why you think the people are resting in these places. All right?
Candidate A	*[1 minute.]*
Interlocutor	Thank you. *(Candidate B)*, do you ever go to the gym? (Why? / Why not?)
Candidate B	*[Approximately 30 seconds.*]
Interlocutor	Thank you.

B Enjoying music

Interlocutor	Now, (Candidate B), here are your photographs. They show people enjoying music in different ways. *Indicate the pictures on page 171 to the candidates.* I'd like you to compare the photographs, and say what you think the people are enjoying about their music. All right?
Candidate B	*[1 minute.]*
Interlocutor	Thank you. *(Candidate A)*, would you like to write music? (Why?)
Candidate A	*[Approximately 30 seconds.]*
Interlocutor	Thank you.

Part 3	4 minutes (5 minutes for groups of three)
Part 4	4 minutes (6 minutes for groups of three)

Part 3 Qualifications

Interlocutor	Now, I'd like you to talk about something together for about two minutes (*3 minutes for groups of three*). Some people think that in order to be successful, it's important to get qualifications in lots of different subjects. Here are some things they think about and a question for you to discuss. First you have some time to look at the task. *Indicate the text on page 172 to the candidates. Allow 15 seconds.* Now, talk to each other about whether it's important to get lots of different qualifications if you want to be successful.
Candidates	*[2 minutes (3 minutes for groups of three).]*
Interlocutor	Thank you. Now you have about a minute to decide what the best reason is for getting lots of different qualifications.
Candidates	*[1 minute (for pairs and groups of three).]*
Interlocutor	Thank you.

Part 4

Interlocutor Use the following questions, in order, as appropriate:

- Do you enjoy learning new things that could be useful in the future? (Why? / Why not?)
- Do you think it's a good idea for students to have a part-time job when they're studying at college or university? (Why? / Why not?)
- Some people say that the only reason for getting good qualifications is to get a good job. What do you think? (Why?)
- Do you think that people have to work too hard these days? (Why? / Why not?)
- Do you think it's a good idea for people to work in another country for a while? (Why? / Why not?)
- Some people say that money is the most important thing to think about when you're choosing a career. Do you agree? (Why? / Why not?)

Select any of the following prompts, as appropriate:

- What do you think?
- Do you agree?
- And you?

Thank you. That is the end of the test.

Test 4

Note: The visual material for Test 4 appears on pages 173–175.

Part 1
2 minutes (3 minutes for groups of three)

Interlocutor

Good morning/afternoon/evening. My name is .... and this is my colleague ....
And your names are?
Can I have your mark sheets, please?
Thank you.

- Where are you from, *(Candidate A)*?
- And you, *(Candidate B)*?

First, we'd like to know something about you.

Select one or more questions from any of the following categories, as appropriate.

Family and friends

- Who are you most like in your family? (In what ways are you similar?)
- Do you go on holiday with your family? (Why? / Why not?)
- Have you done anything interesting with your friends recently? (What did you do with them?)
- Tell me about a really good friend of yours. (Do you share the same interests?)

Your interests

- Is there a sport or hobby you enjoy doing? (What do you do?) (Why do you like it?)
- If you could learn a new skill, what would you choose to do? (Why?)
- Do you like reading? (What do you read?) (Why do you like it?)
- Have you seen a good film recently? (Tell me about it.)

Future plans

- Have you got any plans for this weekend? (What are you going to do?)
- Are you going to go on holiday this year? (Where are you going to go?)
- Is there anything you'd like to study in the future? (Why?)
- Which country would you most like to visit in the future? (Do you think you'll go there one day?) (Why? / Why not?)

Part 2
4 minutes (6 minutes for groups of three)

A Preparing food

Interlocutor	In this part of the test, I'm going to give each of you two photographs. I'd like you to talk about your photographs on your own for about a minute, and also to answer a question about your partner's photographs. *(Candidate A)*, it's your turn first. Here are your photographs. They show people preparing food in different situations. *Indicate the pictures on page 173 to the candidates.* I'd like you to compare the photographs, and say why you think the people are preparing food in these situations. All right?
Candidate A	*[1 minute.]*
Interlocutor	Thank you. *(Candidate B)*, do you like cooking for your family and friends? (Why? / Why not?)
Candidate B	*[Approximately 30 seconds.]*
Interlocutor	Thank you.

B Writing

Interlocutor	Now, *(Candidate B)*, here are your photographs. They show people writing in different situations. *Indicate the pictures on page 174 to the candidates.* I'd like you to compare the photographs, and say why you think the people are writing in these situations. All right?
Candidate B	*[1 minute.]*
Interlocutor	Thank you. *(Candidate A)*, do you find it easy to study at home? (Why? / Why not?)
Candidate A	*[Approximately 30 seconds.]*
Interlocutor	Thank you.

Part 3	4 minutes (5 minutes for groups of three)
Part 4	4 minutes (6 minutes for groups of three)

Part 3 Advertising

Interlocutor	Now, I'd like you to talk about something together for about two minutes (*3 minutes for groups of three*). Some people believe that they are too easily influenced by advertising. Here are some things they think about and a question for you to discuss. First you have some time to look at the task. *Indicate the text on page 175 to the candidates. Allow 15 seconds.* Now, talk to each other about whether people are too easily influenced by advertising.
Candidates	*[2 minutes (3 minutes for groups of three).]*
Interlocutor	Thank you. Now you have about a minute to decide which is the best reason for not watching any advertisements.
Candidates	*[1 minute (for pairs and groups of three).]*
Interlocutor	Thank you.

Part 4

Interlocutor

Use the following questions, in order, as appropriate:

- Do you enjoy watching adverts on television? (Why? / Why not?)
- Some people say that there should be no adverts for children's toys on television. What do you think? (Why?)
- Some people say that we can learn more about products from talking to friends than watching advertising. What do you think? (Why?)
- Do you think that advertising always tells us the truth about a product? (Why? / Why not?)
- Do you think people go shopping just because of the advertisements they've seen? (Why? / Why not?)
- Do you think that in the future people will do most of their shopping online? (Why? / Why not?)

Select any of the following prompts, as appropriate:

- What do you think?
- Do you agree?
- And you?

Thank you. That is the end of the test.

Sample Writing answers

Additional sample Writing answers in Resource bank

Sample A (Test 1, Question 1 – Essay)

If you stop from whatever you're doing, and look, just for a second, you'll realize that life is pretty wonderful. So, why not makning everyone feel this beauty and be proud of it?

Helping other people is not about them, is about you. You feel that energy whenever you do something nice. Benig knid costs you nothing, more than that, you get to win from it. I like thinkning that this Universe is a circle, and everythning you do, in a weird manner, comes back to you.

Family and friends are the thing that defines us. Everyone should be your friend and everyone should be your family. You love them, right? Your close ones? You love them so much, that you don't even realize what would you do for them. So why not (help not) helpning the rest of humanity in the same way? It won't hurt us, it may actually help us.

Everyone lives in a city, in a country, so you have a society that you're in, something that helpes you have a decent life. By helpning people you add something, you pay your contribution to the ones that make this world have a sense, rules. You help them because it's clearly that they've once helped you.

So, for one minute, go outside, stand there in silence, and contemplate how amazing the life is. That's what helping people does to you.

Subscale	Mark	Commentary
Content	5	All content is relevant to the task. The target reader is fully informed as the two points in the task have been covered, and the writer has included their own idea explaining what benefits can be felt when people help others: *You feel that energy when you do something nice; everythning you do, in a weird manner, comes back to you.*
Communicative Achievement	5	The conventions of an essay, such as expressing opinions, justifying a certain position and presenting different sides of an argument, are used effectively. Rhetorical questions addressed directly to the reader are engaging and hold the target reader's attention: *So, why not makning everyone feel this beauty and be proud of it? You love them, right? Your close ones?; So why not ….* Both straightforward and some more complex ideas are expressed: *I like thinkning that this Universe is a circle, and everythning you do, in a weird manner, comes back to you.*
Organisation	4	The text is well organised and coherent. There are clear paragraphs, each one containing a separate idea, and there are cohesive devices, such as repetition, relative pronouns, paraphrasing and simple linking words, used throughout the text to connect the ideas both within and across sentences: *is not about them is about you. You …; more than that; your family. You love them, right? Your close ones; So why not …; go outside, stand there … and.*

Language	5	The writer uses a range of vocabulary, including some less common lexis and collocations, appropriately to express some complex ideas: *pretty wonderful; be proud; feel that energy; costs you nothing; Universe; weird; defines; Your close ones; humanity; decent life; contribution; contemplate*. There is a range of simple and complex grammatical forms used with control and some flexibility to communicate specific ideas: *Benig knid costs you nothing, more than that, you get to win from it; You love them so much, that you don't even realize what would you do for them; It may actually help; So, for one minute, go outside, stand there in silence, and contemplate how amazing the life is*. There are errors, mainly with spelling and words ending in 'ing', but these do not impede: *makning; Benig; knid; thinkning; everythning; helpning*.

Sample B (Test 1, Question 2 – Report)

Cycling facilities are the best solution for people, who want to cycle in amusing places. They can ensure, that you have a pleasant experience while cycling.

There are a lot of cycling facilities to choose from. Some of them are of more quality than others, but all of the facilities in my area should provide great fun to those who use them.

The cyclists in my town are not easyly pleased with places they might want to visit. A popular place to cycle in is the city park. A lot of people come here to train their legs and admire the nature around them. Another popular place is a cycling track in the rural part of the town. Here you can cycle for a long distance not disturbed by noise pollution.

Cycling in this area is really fun but sometimes dangerous. In order to make it safer the cycling track should be rebuilt. This way noone will fall over the edge. Another option is to put up road signs prohibiting from entering dangerous areas. It is not a satisfying solution, but an efafective one.

Subscale	Mark	Commentary
Content	4	All content is relevant to the task. The target reader is on the whole informed. The second and third points, where cyclists can use their bikes and how cycling can be made safer in the area, are fully covered. However, although the first point, explaining about the available facilities, is attempted, there is a lack of detail to fully explain what the facilities are: *There are a lot of cycling facilities to choose from. Some of them are of more quality than others, but all of the facilities in my area should provide great fun to those who use them*.
Communicative Achievement	3	The conventions of a report, such as giving factual information in an objective way, are used to communicate straightforward ideas. Although it is not a typical report format with headings, the information is presented clearly and in such a way as to inform, and the tone and register are consistent, which helps to hold the target reader's attention.
Organisation	4	The report is well organised and coherent, despite the lack of headings. Topic sentences are used to introduce each point, and further information is then added using paraphrasing to avoid too much repetition: *A popular place to cycle in is the city park … Another popular place is … Here ….* There are some cohesive devices, such as relative pronouns, used to link the ideas across paragraphs: *Cycling in this area is really fun but sometimes dangerous. In order to make it*.
Language	3	The writer uses a range of everyday vocabulary related to cycling appropriately with some attempts to use less common lexis: *amusing places; pleasant experiences; easyly pleased; admire; rural part; noise pollution; cycling track; prohibiting; satisfying solution*. There is a range of simple and some complex grammatical forms, such as modal verbs and passive forms, which are used with a good degree of control: *should be rebuilt; Another option is to put up road signs prohibiting*. There are a few errors, mainly spelling and punctuation, but these do not impede communication: *they can ensure, that you; easyly*.

Sample C (Test 2, Question 1 – Essay)

In my opinion, students should have to do sport at school and I'm going to explain why.

The most important thing about sport is learning new skills. In your futur life, you'll mabye have to work with colleges. Therefore, if you have learnt teamwork at school, you would be able to work easier. In addition, learning skills like how to play football will always be in your favour.

On the overhand, there are some people who hate sport. They don't like running because it's boring, ect.

Peraps, they are just lazy or prefer playing an instrument, painting or singing.

Finally, doing sport is a great way to keep fit and healthy. It's an adventage if you look good in your mind and body. Sport help you realax and better in your life.

Overall, doing sport at school makes you learn new skills like teamwork, makes you feel better even though some people hate that.

Subscale	Mark	Commentary
Content	5	All content is relevant to the task. The target reader is fully informed as the two points in the task have been covered and the writer's own idea, being fit and healthy, is discussed.
Communicative Achievement	3	The conventions of an essay, such as an objective tone and a neutral register, have been used to communicate straightforward ideas. The target reader's attention is held due to the development of the main points and the explanations which are given to support the writer's point of view: *if you have learnt teamwork at school, you would be able to work easier*.
Organisation	3	The text is generally well organised and paragraphs have been used to separate the main points. There is some use of cohesive devices at the beginning of sentences, which helps to connect the ideas throughout the text and which provide a structure to the text overall: *In my opinion; The most important thing; Therefore; In addition; On the overhand; Finally; Overall*.
Language	3	The writer uses a range of everyday vocabulary which is relevant to the topic, and which is used appropriately: *skills; running; lazy; playing an instrument; fit and healthy; mind and body*. There is a range of simple and some more complex grammatical forms, such as forms of the present, conditional clauses and modal verbs, which are used with a good degree of control: *If you have learnt … you would be able to*. There are a few errors, but these do not impede communication: *work with colleges; on the overhand; Peraps; adventage; realax*.

Sample D (Test 2, Question 3 – Article)

The most useful advice I have ever recive was from my grandmother and it is sound like this 'You will never fully belive in yourself if you keep comparing yourself with everyone else' and I found that she was right. Every time I have comparing myself with someone else I lost my confidence.

This advice is very useful because it would help you. Why to comparing yourself with everyone else when you can comparing with yourself? I think this would be the best way to improve yourself, your personality and your ability.

The risk in compare with someone else is that would maybe you choose the wrong person.

In conclusion, my grandmother advice is very useful to me because it change my life. I develop my confidence in my self and now I didn't do that anymore.

Subscale	Mark	Commentary
Content	5	All content is relevant to the task. The target reader is fully informed about the advice which was given and why it was so useful to the writer.
Communicative Achievement	4	The conventions of an article, such as a personal perspective and language of description and explanation, are used effectively to communicate some complex ideas. The target reader's attention is held due to the nature of the advice given and the personal view explained within the text.
Organisation	3	The text is generally well organised. There is a clear, logical structure to the text and the main ideas are presented in a coherent manner. There is some use of linking words and a few cohesive devices to connect the sentences and paragraphs, but these are limited due to the length of the text, which affects how many examples there are: *The most useful advice; This advice; In conclusion.*
Language	3	The writer uses everyday vocabulary, which is related to the task, in an appropriate way: *belive in yourself; lost my confidence; improve yourself, your personality and your ability; risk; develop my confidence.* There is some range of grammatical structures, such as modal verbs and comparative structures: *if you keep comparing yourself with everyone else; I think this would be the best way to.* However, when more complex ideas or structures are attempted, such as present perfect, errors occur, but these do not impede communication: *I have ever recive; it is sound like; I have comparing; why to comparing; The risk in compare; now I didn't do that.*

Sample E (Test 3, Question 1 – Essay)

Advertising is in today's medialized world an important albeit annoying part of everyday life. The majority of it is aimed at adults with steady incomes but still, few are aimed at their children. Most ads aimed at children are very captivating with happy tunes and bright pastel colors making use of the childrens' short attention span. Children find this wonderful and are often happy when they see their favourite commercial in the television or the smiling mascot of their favourite brand.

This kind of advertising presents a burden for the parents, as they have to spend money for an unnecessary toys and thing the child would do without.

In my opinion, advertising as it is can be easily abolished, as today's people already mostly know what they want and sometimes even children.

Children nowadays express great interest in things not made for them, such as electronics or video games, making their marketing towards children unnecessary and even looked down upon.

Subscale	Mark	Commentary
Content	5	All content is relevant to the task. The target reader is fully informed. The two points in the task are mentioned and developed and the writer's own idea, the inappropriateness of some of the adverts aimed at children, is briefly mentioned at the end of the essay.
Communicative Achievement	5	The conventions of an essay, such as an objective tone and a formal register, as well as an appropriate format consisting of an introduction, discussion and a conclusion, are used effectively to communicate straightforward and some more complex ideas. The writer provides examples of how adverts are viewed differently by different groups of people and what effect this has.
Organisation	5	The text is well organised and coherent. The essay structure is clear and the points are presented in separate paragraphs, which help the reader to locate the information. Cohesive devices, such as referencing and paraphrasing to avoid repetition, are used to generally good effect: *an important albeit annoying; advertising … ads … commercial … marketing; This kind of*.
Language	4	The writer uses a range of vocabulary, including some more formal expressions, which are suitable for the task: *albeit; aimed at adults with steady incomes; captivating; bright pastel colours; short attention span; mascot; burden; abolished*. There is a range of simple grammatical forms used with a good degree of control, but errors occur when trying to express some more complex ideas with higher level structures: *advertising as it is can be easily abolished, as today's people already mostly know what they want and sometimes even children; making their marketing towards children unnecessary and even looked down upon*. However, the message is still communicated despite the errors.

Sample F (Test 3, Question 2 – Email)

Hello Nick.

That is actually really tough situation. This decision can change your future at all.

But as a very experienced student, I would strongly recomment you to choose history. It is very interesting topic, you can choose the time period that fits you the best and inspires you the most.

You can't even imagine all the battles, defences and many other interesting things that happened. This can change your opinion on your actual life.

On the other hand, literature and engineering are not bad choices either. Plus literature is closly connected with history; In some writings, many of the battles are mentioned. Maybe you should combine these two.

I hope I gave you some ideas to think of and it helped you at least a bit. And I hope you will not regret your decision later. All these subjects sound fun and are usuful in life.

I wish you the best of luck! Have a nice day.

Saša.

Subscale	Mark	Commentary
Content	5	All content is relevant to the task. The target reader is fully informed as the writer has given an opinion on each subject and suggested which one would be most suitable.
Communicative Achievement	4	The conventions of an email to a friend, such as a friendly tone and an informal register, as well as appropriate opening and closing salutations, are used effectively to communicate straightforward ideas: *Hello Nick; You can't even imagine; I hope I gave you; And I hope you will not regret your decision; I wish you the best of luck; Have a nice day.* The target reader's attention is held due to the nature of the advice given and the relevance to the situation.
Organisation	4	The text is well organised and coherent. The input material is referred to but the information is not repeated: *That is actually really tough situation*, and the ideas in the email are presented in a logical order. Cohesive devices are used to link the ideas both within and across sentences and paragraphs: *This decision; many other interesting things; On the other hand … either; Plus; combine these two; these subjects*. The writer uses a range of everyday vocabulary related to the topic of study and the specific subjects mentioned: *experienced student; topic; time period; inspires; battles, defences; writings; regret*.
Language	3	There is a range of grammatical structures including some more complex forms, used with a good degree of control, such as verb and plural agreement: *you can choose the time period that fits you the best and inspires you the most; literature and engineering are not bad choices either; many of the battles are mentioned; And I hope you will not regret your decision later*. There are a few errors, but these do not impede communication.

Sample G (Test 4, Question 1 – Essay)

> *Is it better to be part of a large family or a small family?*
>
> *That seems to be a fairly easy question, but is it really? Both of these options have their advantages and their disadvantages. This essay will consider both of these options.*
>
> *In general, the cost of living is lower in a smaller family than in a bigger one, simply because the money doesn't need to be divided between many family members.*
>
> *It is believed that having siblings is an advantage when it comes to learning from others. You learn to share and to deal with people, which is important.*
>
> *In my opinion, having a big family is an advantage when we look for a job. It is much easier to find one through a family member than on your own.*
>
> *In conclusion, being part of a small family can be both good and bad for you, and the same goes for a large family. It all depends on your personality and your social skills.*

Subscale	Mark	Commentary
Content	5	All content is relevant to the task. The target reader is fully informed. The two points in the task are discussed and developed and the writer includes their own idea, which involves the ease of getting a job if a person has a large family.
Communicative Achievement	4	The conventions of an essay, such as an objective tone and a formal register when introducing and discussing ideas, are used effectively. Straightforward ideas are presented and the target reader's attention is held due to the focus on one idea in each section of text. The use of rhetorical questions engages the reader's interest and the writer's opinions are clearly stated.
Organisation	4	The text is generally well organised and coherent. There is a variety of appropriate cohesive devices used to introduce ideas and to link them through the text: *Both of these; In general; simply because; In my opinion; In conclusion; can be both; and the same goes for*.
Language	4	The writer uses a range of everyday vocabulary appropriately, including some accurate collocations: *cost of living; divided; siblings; share; deal with; personality; social skills*. There is a range of grammatical forms used with control and some flexibility, particularly when contrasting information: *It is much easier to find one through a family member than on your own*. The text is practically error free.

Sample H (Test 4, Question 3 – Letter of application)

8th October

Dear organizer,

I have been reading the article about the trip you are organising, and it seems to be really enjoyable. In fact, I am very interested by it. I am a passionate traveller, and I have already made kind of trips like it but I am much more interested about Artic, where I never went. These are a list of subjective abilities I have that could be useful for the trip.

Firstly, as I said, I have already been confronted to long expseditions like it. For the language, I am born in France, but I went 5 years to England so I am practicly english speaker and I believe the England winter cold is much harder then artic. (:))

Secondly, for such a destination, we should absolutely stick together, and I have always been a team work personn, only because I believe that team work is the solution to hard work.

However, I think that I might have some skills for this environment. I know how to fish into ice, how to hunt, so I have a little bit of experiment in what to do in hand situation; I also know how to climb ice due to Iceland and learned how to make fire with sticks.

Finally I hope you took note of my motivation to be a part of you're adventure. Thank if you let me be a part of it.

Kind regards,

Subscale	Mark	Commentary
Content	5	All content is relevant to the task. The target reader is fully informed about the skills the writer has, their ability to work in a team and what their level of English is.
Communicative Achievement	3	The conventions of a letter of application, such as suitable opening and closing salutations, as well as a persuasive tone and mostly consistent register, are used to communicate straightforward ideas, and the target reader's attention is held: *Dear organizer; In fact, I am very interested by it; Kind regards*
Organisation	2	The text is generally well organised, making good use of paragraphs to focus on separate aspects of the task. There is some use of linking words to order the information both within sentences and at the beginning of paragraphs: *and; but; so; because; Firstly; Secondly; Finally*, but these are quite simple. The use of *However* is not quite right as the purpose of the paragraph is to add further information rather than contrast with what has gone before.
Language	3	There is a range of everyday vocabulary which is suitable for the task: *enjoyable; passionate; destination; stick together; fish into ice; hunt; climb ice; make fire with sticks; motivation*. The grammatical structures are mainly quite simple, mainly present tenses and one-clause sentences, but there is some attempt to use more complex structures at times: *Secondly, for such a destination and time, we should absolutely stick together, and I have always been a team work personn.* There are a number of errors with spelling, and wrong word choices, but generally these do not impede communication: *where I never went; subjective abilities; confronted to long expseditions; practicly; artic.*

Test 1 answer key

Reading and Use of English

Answer key with extra explanations in Resource bank

Part 1

1 C **2** D **3** A **4** B **5** D **6** C **7** B **8** B

Part 2

9 far **10** to **11** such **12** why **13** When **14** was
15 like **16** nothing

Part 3

17 variety **18** innovative/innovatory **19** blindness **20** experimental
21 assistant(s) **22** arrangement(s) **23** memorable **24** unforgettable

Part 4

25 AS long as | I (can)
26 can run NO | further/farther/more than
27 mean/intend to spend | SO much
28 me NEVER to | run unless
29 CLEAR explanation | of
30 off | OWING to

Part 5

31 C **32** A **33** B **34** B **35** D **36** B

Part 6

37 D **38** A **39** E **40** G **41** F **42** C

Part 7

43 B **44** C **45** D **46** A **47** C **48** B **49** A **50** B **51** C **52** A

Listening

Answer key with extra explanations in Resource bank

Part 1

1 A **2** B **3** A **4** A **5** C **6** B **7** A **8** C

Part 2

9 International Conservation Garden **10** donkey **11** Medicine **12** storms **13** bicycle/bike **14** growth **15** shelters **16** (the) (ancient/old) villages **17** terrace **18** sun(-)cream

Part 3

19 E **20** F **21** B **22** H **23** D

Part 4

24 B **25** C **26** A **27** A **28** C **29** A **30** C

Audioscript

Test One.

I am going to give you the instructions for this test. I shall introduce each part of the test and give you time to look at the questions. At the start of each piece you will hear this sound:

tone

You will hear each piece twice.

Remember, while you are listening, write your answers on the question paper. You will have five minutes at the end of the test to copy your answers onto the separate answer sheet.

There will now be a pause. Please ask any questions now, because you must not speak during the test.

[pause]

Now open your question paper and look at Part One.

[pause]

PART 1 *You will hear people talking in eight different situations. For questions 1 to 8, choose the best answer (A, B or C).*

Question 1 *You hear a woman talking about learning to play the piano.*

[pause]

tone

Woman: Learning to play the piano is far harder than I'd imagined when I started. You really can't improve unless you practise. I'm hopeless at that, but after all, I have a busy life, and this is just a hobby. However, it's one I enjoy, and the time I can spend doing it is precious. So while I admit I'm still playing very basic, easy pieces, and playing them pretty poorly at that, the little progress I have made encourages me to keep on going to lessons. My teacher's very patient, fortunately, and never makes me feel bad, so maybe I'll finally be able to impress my friends one day!

[pause]

tone

[The recording is repeated.]

[pause]

Question 2 *You hear a woman telling a friend about having a celebration dinner.*

[pause]

tone

Man: Did you have a good weekend?

Woman: Yes, it was my sister's birthday and we cooked a meal for everyone. Cooking for other people can be so stressful. It had seemed a good idea to try a new recipe, and I'd got the ingredients ready in advance. I managed to forget ginger though, so the stir-fry was lacking a vital ingredient, but it didn't seem to matter. I always make way too much, so I had no concerns about people going hungry. Still, it was great that the conversation flowed so well, and in fact nobody seemed to want to leave. There was loads of clearing up though.

[pause]

tone

[The recording is repeated.]

[pause]

Question 3 *You hear a man telling a friend about a visit to a museum.*

[pause]

tone

Woman: Did you enjoy your visit to the museum last week?

Man: I did, thanks. You know how much I'd been looking forward to it – well, it lived up to all my expectations. As you know, they've just renovated the whole building, and it really is great. There's an exhibition on of paintings of the countryside around here. It made me realise I'd really like to do something like that too, so I've signed up for a beginner's painting course.

Woman: Great! And was the museum busy?

Man: Oh, yes – I've heard the place is permanently packed these days. I thought it would've been quiet on a Monday.

[pause]

tone

[The recording is repeated.]

[pause]

Question 4 *You hear two media students talking about a TV advert they have seen.*

[pause]

tone

Man: Did you see the advert for that new health drink?

Woman: I did, but I thought it was all pretty predictable … you know, bright smiley faces ... young woman leaping about in slow motion ...

Man: Yes, there wasn't a great deal of novelty, was there? But then again, is there ever in an advert for a fruit drink? It was certainly technically very good, wasn't it? Well-designed …

Woman: Short and snappy … made its point effectively. Not sure how believable the leaping woman was, though ... you know, the suggestion that if you drink it, you immediately come over all energetic.

Man: But surely you weren't meant to take that literally.

[pause]

tone

[The recording is repeated.]

[pause]

Question 5 *You hear two people talking about a work colleague called Judy.*

[pause]

tone

Man: Have you heard that Judy's leaving?

Woman: Yeah ... such a lovely person.

Man: I think she never really recovered from the disappointment of being overlooked for that promotion. Seemed to hit her hard, and she was the obvious person for the job, let's be honest.

Woman: In many ways she deserved it, sure. But Gavin, who got the job, was … kind of more obviously committed, don't you think?

Man: Very energetic, yes. Judy was quieter, I guess … she went about her daily business with no fuss. And what she did, she did very efficiently, so you could rely on her work being free of mistakes, which is very important in our line of business.

[pause]

tone

[The recording is repeated.]

[pause]

Question 6 *You hear two friends talking about a local project to start a community garden.*

[pause]

tone

Woman: Are you coming to the meeting tomorrow? We're going to discuss the design of the community garden.

Man: No, community projects aren't my thing. Everyone starts off being really enthusiastic and then one by one they all drop out, and so all the work falls on a couple of people. I've seen it happen so many times. And where are the plants coming from?

Woman: All the plants, the land and equipment is being provided free of charge by the local council. The residents are really keen and we've elected a committee to run things too.

Man: Let's talk again in six months' time and see if it's still on track!

[pause]

tone

[The recording is repeated.]

[pause]

Question 7 *You hear two friends discussing watching films based on books.*

[pause]

tone

Woman: Do you fancy going to see *Trapped* at the cinema tomorrow? I really enjoyed reading the book.

Man: I don't know how you can watch a film after you've read the book. I'd hate it if the film wasn't faithful to the storyline.

Woman: Yes, but once you're right into the film, you forget about that. It's only later that you think – oh hang on, that didn't happen in the book! I think you miss so much if you haven't read it. You don't know the inner thoughts of the characters or their motivation for doing things. It doesn't matter how good the director is, some things just can't be brought to the screen.

Man: Mmm.

[pause]

tone

[The recording is repeated.]

[pause]

Question 8 *You hear a man telling a friend about a new sports centre.*

[pause]

tone

Woman: So did you enjoy your visit to the new sports centre in town?

Man: Yes. I went for a swim and had a look round the gym.

Woman: Only a look round?

Man: Yes. I hadn't realised, but you have to become a member to use the gym.

Woman: But anyone can swim?

Man: Yes, or even use the athletics track. But they said the gym isn't open access … they want everyone to have an induction programme to show them how to use the machines safely. With the track, there's an athletics club you can join if you want to get coaching and all that, but you don't have to ... that's the difference.

[pause]

tone

[The recording is repeated.]

[pause]

That is the end of Part One.

Now turn to Part Two.

[pause]

PART 2

You will hear a student called Petra Dean talking about her recent work experience as a volunteer in the Cloud Forest in Ecuador in South America. For questions 9 to 18, complete the sentences with a word or short phrase.

You now have forty-five seconds to look at Part Two.

[pause]

tone

Hello, my name's Petra Dean and I'd like to tell you about my amazing trip to the Cloud Forest in Ecuador in South America. I volunteered there for a month last summer on the Cloud Forest Project.

I'm a postgraduate student now and my first degree was in Biology. While I was doing that, I realised that I wanted to continue my studies but specialise more – so I chose International Conservation, which I love doing. Going to Ecuador was a way for me to get in some practical experience.

When I arrived in Ecuador, I spent my first night in a hostel in the capital, Quito. The next day I set off for the nature reserve, which is situated in the Cloud Forest. The journey began with a three-hour bus ride out into the countryside. The second part was more unexpected. A donkey was the designated mode of transport up the steep forest paths to the reserve!

The reserve had its own farm, and at first I was assigned to work in the two gardens. The one which they called the Medicine Garden was where plants that can be used to treat illness were grown – it gave me a real buzz to know that I was growing plants for research that might heal people. The other was the organic vegetable garden where we grew our own delicious fruit and vegetables.

The weather was perfect for doing outside work. I was there during the rainy season, so the temperatures were very comfortable. There were storms each evening and they were really dramatic to watch. We were surrounded by the most amazing mountains, but for days on end they weren't visible due to the blanket of cloud that descended over the forest.

There were goats on the reserve, and one of my tasks was taking the milk down to the nearest village every day, which wasn't much fun. The barrels of fresh milk were loaded onto a bicycle and I had to steer it down the steep paths. It was exhausting because it seemed to have a mind of its own! When I got to the village, the milk was loaded into a rickety old lorry for the rest of the way down the mountain.

One aspect of the programme that I really appreciated was the forestry programme. Volunteers had to assist in collecting and planting seeds, maintaining the plant nursery and – my particular task – conducting forest inventories. That involved assessing the trees' growth. This provided invaluable information for scientists trying to learn about what's going on in the forest.

It wasn't all work though. We also had the chance to get to know the forest better. The local people taught us about the trees that are native to the area. We also had a mini-survival course and were instructed on the best way to put up shelters high up in the branches. Our guides showed us edible plants, but I found it impossible to identify them.

There was plenty of free time at the weekends. A friend and I spent one weekend cycling through the countryside, stopping off to explore the ruins of ancient villages. I'll never forget that! Over the next few weekends, we visited the nearby towns and saw the local sites of historical interest, which were surprisingly free of crowds as it was outside the tourist season.

The volunteer house had everything you could want – cold showers, electricity and comfortable bedrooms to unwind in after a long day of physical exertion. Then, after a delicious dinner of home-grown food served in the dining room, I wanted nothing more than to sit out on the terrace and listen to the sounds of the wildlife. That was just magical.

I can honestly say that I wouldn't change a thing about this experience. Oh, OK, maybe one thing … I packed a mosquito net, insect spray and, of course, sun cream as suggested – but nowhere near enough. It was surprisingly hard to come by while I was there, and it was very expensive. But despite all that, I would say that it really was the trip of a lifetime!

[pause]

Now you will hear Part Two again.

tone

[The recording is repeated.]

[pause]

That is the end of Part Two.

Now turn to Part Three.

[pause]

PART 3

You will hear five short extracts in which people talk about their jobs on a cruise ship. For questions 19 to 23, choose from the list (A to H) what each speaker says about working on a cruise ship. Use the letters only once. There are three extra letters which you do not need to use.

You now have thirty seconds to look at Part Three.

[pause]

tone

Speaker 1

I work in the front office on board ship, answering passenger queries and so on. I used to work in the back office but I wanted to better myself, so I took some customer service evening courses at my local college between cruises and then re-applied for work on the ship. That's what's good about this line of work – you can move up quite quickly. What I love about this job is that you really get to interact with passengers. We get people from all walks of life – lots of couples, but families too. They come for the holiday of a lifetime – a bit of luxury – and why not?

[pause]

Speaker 2

There's a common misconception that everyone who works on a cruise ship is in their early twenties but most people here are older than me. I was going nowhere professionally, so thought I'd try my hand here. Most of the cruise singers – myself included – dream of being 'discovered' by a passenger who also happens to be a record producer – a bit unlikely I know! The staff quarters are brilliant – my cabin is better than my bedroom back home! And the social life is great too. We have some fantastic staff parties and we even put on our own concerts sometimes!

[pause]

Speaker 3

Well, I'm a bit of an oddity actually because I'm a whole lot older than most people who work onboard. I'm 68! Also, I don't get paid! That's right! Many people ask me why I do it, but I have the chance to go on all these wonderful cruises for absolutely nothing! My role is to accompany the groups when they go ashore and make sure everything runs smoothly. It's perfect! I spend all my time with the passengers, and I've made some lovely friends over the years. My husband does the same thing, but it's a shame it's on another ship, though. At least we have lots to talk about!

[pause]

Speaker 4

I'm a chef. Catering is hard work – it's really full on most of the time. Some nights I can't wait to get back to the cabin and put my feet up, even if the space is a bit small! My wife's a childminder onboard, and although we work completely different hours, it's ideal really 'cos otherwise I wouldn't see much of her. I qualified and worked in a restaurant in Canada, but I always wanted to travel. It's not a luxurious lifestyle for the staff onboard but the job does allow me to see new places.

[pause]

Speaker 5

[pause]

I work in the tour office organising the tours that the passengers can go on when we make our various stops. Although the pay isn't great – especially as we don't make any tips like they do in the restaurant – there are other perks. <u>There are like loads of courses we can do. I've learnt Italian and brushed up my computer skills</u> since I've been doing this job. The staff social activities are fantastic – almost as good as the passengers' entertainment! On the whole, the passengers are really nice. I mean, I love seeing them all dressed up in their posh clothes going in for dinner!

[pause]

Now you will hear Part Three again.

tone

[The recording is repeated.]

[pause]

That is the end of Part Three.

Now turn to Part Four.

[pause]

PART 4 *You will hear an interview with a man called Guy Riordan, who works as a stuntman performing dangerous scenes in movies. For questions 24 to 30, choose the best answer (A, B or C).*

You now have one minute to look at Part Four.

[pause]

tone

Interviewer: When you see a fight or a car chase in a movie, it's often a stuntman or woman taking the risks – not a real actor! Guy Riordan's a top stuntman. Guy, do you usually work individually or in a team?

Guy: It depends … in my first job I was part of a team of other stuntmen ... several of us had to jump off a fourth-floor rooftop together and get caught by the group on the ground. <u>That involved relying on everyone else to do things properly, which wasn't something I enjoyed!</u> Despite that uncertainty, I hoped my strength and sense of timing would get me through. Audiences rarely appreciate the lengths we go to to provide their entertainment!

Interviewer: Obviously it's dangerous, but what's the most challenging thing for you about the work?

Guy: It's a wonderful job, but like any career, you have to have tools – for a stuntman, it's his or her body – and if a stunt goes wrong, you can end up badly hurt. If I thought about that, though, I'd never do the job. <u>But it's the never-ending process to up your game, to expand and extend what you're good at – that's the toughest bit.</u> Of course, there's a lot of competition in the stunt world – that makes it exciting.

Interviewer: What was it like working on the movie *Raw Stuff*?

Guy: It's based on a true story about soldiers in action, so it was extremely important that the stunts didn't look like standard movie action sequences. The mountains we were filming in were stunning, which made up for having to hike up with 25 kilos of equipment on our backs … you just didn't notice the weight! The view from the top was sensational. <u>The tricky part was tumbling onto rocky mountain ledges</u> so that the camera could be as close as possible, and the audiences would see and feel what those soldiers went through.

Interviewer: You've often acted as a stunt double for the actor Marty Walker …

Guy: Yeah, Marty and I get on. He varies his size drastically from one movie to the next – <u>he can go from athletic action hero to skinny professor in some major body transformations. His dedication to doing that's amazing.</u> It affects me as well … I had to put on weight for his last movie. Marty wanted to do the motorbike stunts himself, but we persuaded him not to. It involved jumping off at high speed … pretty silly for an untrained person to try and do, or even a stuntman …

Interviewer: Which movie do you remember filming most?

Guy: *Light at Dawn*. They wanted me to say some lines – real acting. After a few attempts I gave up and asked for someone else to do it. The director Peter Levene was very ambitious – some things he asked for hadn't been tried before. <u>It was truly a pleasure when we got things right.</u> We filmed all over the world – everyone on what was a huge film crew was completely exhausted flying from one place to the next!

Interviewer: How long have you been in the movie industry?

Guy: Twenty years. I've seen some changes. There's more technology these days, but there's just as great a need for stunt actors. Some things can only be performed by a real human. I've worked with some great people in some great locations – and <u>had a lot of laughs – something that's increasingly missing these days</u> because there's so much at stake. But that does mean the financial rewards for those who get into the big movies are generally worth it. I can't say I've been unlucky in that respect.

Interviewer: What would you advise someone wanting to do your job?

Guy: Stunt work's become highly specialised over the years. There's high falls, fight scenes, horse stunts, car chases, the list goes on. There's no easy answer to the question of whether it's better to become skilled at one thing or be diverse. I don't try and discourage people from getting into stunts, but <u>I do try to convince them to have another source of income to fall back on.</u> Most stuntmen I know also do things like construction, security, web design ... and though everyone has an agent to find them work, it's so often about your own contacts rather than anything else.

[pause]

Now you will hear Part Four again.

tone

[The recording is repeated.]

[pause]

That is the end of Part Four.

There will now be a pause of five minutes for you to copy your answers onto the separate answer sheet. Be sure to follow the numbering of all the questions. I shall remind you when there is one minute left, so that you are sure to finish in time.

[pause – four minutes]

You have one more minute left.

[pause – one minute]

That is the end of the test. Please stop now. Your supervisor will now collect all the question papers and answer sheets.

Test 2 answer key

Reading and Use of English

Answer key with extra explanations in Resource bank

Part 1

1 A **2** B **3** D **4** A **5** C **6** D **7** C **8** A

Part 2

9 which **10** as **11** of **12** its **13** off **14** only
15 anywhere/everywhere **16** to

Part 3

17 outer **18** landing **19** sight **20** boyhood **21** applicants
22 rigorous **23** flight **24** commander

Part 4

25 if/whether I | 'd/would LIKE to
26 get/be in | TOUCH with
27 give/lend me | a (helping) HAND
28 made it | IMPOSSIBLE for
29 FEEL like | coming/going shopping
30 had DIFFICULTY | (in) understanding

Part 5

31 A **32** A **33** C **34** B **35** D **36** B

Part 6

37 F **38** E **39** G **40** A **41** D **42** C

Part 7

43 B **44** A **45** D **46** E **47** A **48** D **49** C **50** E **51** D **52** B

Listening

Answer key with extra explanations in Resource bank

Part 1

1 B **2** C **3** C **4** B **5** A **6** C **7** A **8** B

Part 2

9 February **10** transport **11** Dreams **12** shapes
13 music **14** Box **15** ropes **16** water
17 (rain) curtain **18** sunrise/dawn

Part 3

19 F **20** H **21** E **22** A **23** G

Part 4

24 B **25** A **26** C **27** A **28** B **29** C **30** B

Audioscript

Test Two.

I am going to give you the instructions for this test. I shall introduce each part of the test and give you time to look at the questions. At the start of each piece you will hear this sound:

tone

You will hear each piece twice.

Remember, while you are listening, write your answers on the question paper. You will have five minutes at the end of the test to copy your answers onto the separate answer sheet.

There will now be a pause. Please ask any questions now, because you must not speak during the test.

[pause]

Now open your question paper and look at Part One.

[pause]

PART 1 *You will hear people talking in eight different situations. For questions 1 to 8, choose the best answer (A, B or C).*

Question 1 *You hear a TV presenter talking about making travel documentaries for TV.*

[pause]

tone

Man: I love making travel documentaries for TV. I enjoy the sense of adventure and how travel and meeting other people broadens your horizons. And yet I don't go on holiday … I don't need to. My life is a bit like a holiday, even though I'm actually really busy all the time. My father worked at a job he hated for forty-two years and I remember him saying to me: 'Don't make the mistake I did. Find something you love and make money out of it.' He was so right.

[pause]

tone

[The recording is repeated.]

[pause]

Question 2 *You hear an interview with a woman talking about rowing across the Atlantic Ocean.*

[pause]

tone

Interviewer: Janette, you and your team have just finished rowing across the Atlantic Ocean. What are your feelings?

Woman: It feels like a dream to have arrived. It truly deserves to be called the world's toughest row. We rowed through a hurricane and even got attacked by flying fish! But we are so proud to have achieved something that we originally thought was way beyond our capabilities. We're the oldest team ever to have done it, but that was never an issue for us. Some of the equipment broke, which was what we were really afraid of. But – hey – despite that, we made it!

[pause]

tone

[The recording is repeated.]

[pause]

Question 3 *You hear two colleagues talking about what they did at the weekend.*

[pause]

tone

Man: Good break, Natasha?

Woman: It was OK.

Man: You didn't spend it stuck in front of the computer like you do here in the office?

Woman: I did actually. Well, you know how hard it is for me to keep on top of my workload at the moment. It's really beginning to get me down, so a while ago, I decided I needed a new job. And that's when I realised that most of them require a certificate I haven't got round to getting. <u>So I found the perfect course that I could do online from home.</u> Hardly a break – but at least I feel I'm in a better place now for when I do start going for something new!

[pause]

tone

[The recording is repeated.]

[pause]

Question 4 *You hear an interview with a musician who is talking about being famous.*

[pause]

tone

Man: It's quite strange being famous. When people see me out and about, they often come up to talk. I use the Tube like anyone else who lives in London, and nobody who sees me there tweets 'Why isn't he travelling by helicopter?' because nobody thinks of me like that. People do have an image of me, though – from TV appearances I've made. It's odd to watch the edited version of yourself on TV 'cos I don't look or speak like that normally. <u>There's the adrenaline rush you get when you're on stage that doesn't exist in the rest of your life.</u>

[pause]

tone

[The recording is repeated.]

[pause]

Question 5 *You hear part of an interview with a writer in which he talks about the novel he has written.*

[pause]

tone

Interviewer: You have high hopes for this latest novel of yours, don't you?

Man: I do. It's got everything – action, romance, mystery and a bit of humour. To be honest, if I don't get a phone call from a major studio in the next six months, I'll be very disappointed.

Interviewer: How long did you spend writing it?

Man: Compared to my previous novels, it was relatively painless. The words just flew onto the page and I was all done in about six months. Of course, I know the main character so well by now – it is my third book in the series after all.

[pause]

tone

[The recording is repeated.]

[pause]

Question 6 *You hear a hotel owner talking about her hotel.*

[pause]

tone

Woman: Many people have commented on the customer service in my hotel. They say we're 'smart without being over the top' as some smart hotels are. I think that's a good summary of our whole business model, actually … of everything I believe in. From the start, we took the decision to provide terrific showers and put duvets on the beds – the very best I could find, because that's the way people sleep nowadays. Those are the fundamentals, the basics. It's the same in our restaurants: good food but nothing elitist. But also, to me, real customer service means staff finding that extra five per cent that sets you apart from other hotels.

[pause]

tone

[The recording is repeated.]

[pause]

Question 7 *You hear two friends talking about a housing development scheme in their town.*

[pause]

tone

Woman: I love those new luxury apartments they're building in the city centre. Have you seen them? The restaurants and shops are right on the doorstep.

Man: They're a great addition to the city, I must admit. They add a bit of class to that part of town and they do provide loads of affordable accommodation for single people and couples. They're selling a particular lifestyle, though. There's a real shortage of family accommodation in the city, and these apartments just don't address that. Mind you, at least they don't take up as much space as all those office blocks which seem to dominate the city.

[pause]

tone

[The recording is repeated.]

[pause]

Question 8 *You hear two people on a discussion programme talking about the way employees dress for work.*

[pause]

tone

Man: I heard that most people now believe wearing jeans into the office is acceptable.

Woman: I tend to agree, although there are surely still some professions where only a suit looks presentable – however uncomfortable.

Man: I think the issue of clothes reflects the fact that most business environments are a lot less formal these days. What's more, people are staying later and later in the office, so it's only fair that companies should allow you to dress more comfortably.

Woman: With flexible working hours, focusing on attendance or the way you look isn't considered by bosses to be that important any more. If a job's well done, who cares if it's achieved in a T-shirt?

[pause]

tone

[The recording is repeated.]

[pause]

That is the end of Part One.

Now turn to Part Two.

[pause]

PART 2

You will hear a man called Mark Dawson talking about his visit to the Albuquerque Balloon Festival in New Mexico, USA. For questions 9 to 18, complete the sentences with a word or short phrase.

You now have forty-five seconds to look at Part Two.

[pause]

tone

Hello, everyone. My name is Mark Dawson, and I'd like to tell you about a trip I took to a hot air balloon festival that takes place every year in the United States. It's known as the Albuquerque Balloon Festival.

It's held every October in Albuquerque in New Mexico. Apparently, the first year it took place, in 1974, it was February – but then the organiser realised that from then to April there's the possibility of bad weather, so in 1975 it was moved to later in the year.

The Balloon Festival was started by a businessman. He became very interested in balloons quite by chance. He bought a balloon for a transport company he owned, thinking it would look good in TV advertisements. He loved the experience so much he decided to organise a ballooning event at Albuquerque.

Anyway, the event is held in the desert in New Mexico and the colours and mood of the desert were perfectly reflected in the name of this year's festival – Dreams – last year's was called Up and Away. I was really impressed by the size of the festival when I went. It's actually the largest balloon festival in the world!

The balloons varied in size from absolutely enormous ones that can carry quite a few people to quite small one- or two-person balloons. The colours of the balloons were amazing. The event that drew the biggest crowds of all was specifically for balloons with unconventional shapes such as cartoon characters and even animals.

Another event was called The Flight of the Nations. This is when balloons from all the countries represented at the festival take off one by one while music from their country is played. I really loved this, it was fabulous. This event alone lasted around three hours, and people all around were waving flags.

I was really lucky to bump into a real balloon expert who didn't mind at all when I asked him loads of questions.

Apparently, one reason for the popularity of this balloon festival is something called the Albuquerque Box. It's a unique wind formation caused by the nearby Sandia Mountains and means that if a balloon rides these winds, its path forms a square. This means the pilot is able to land very near the take-off spot.

Looking at the balloons close up, you can see that the balloon part itself is made of really strong, waterproof material. There are ropes that hold the balloon to the basket, and I was told that if something went wrong, you'd cut these, and the basket would fall off and the balloon would turn into a kind of parachute. Not something I'd like to try!

To make the balloon rise up in the air, the pilot has to make it lighter. Now I knew that they often did this by emptying the bags of sand hung on the basket because I'd seen that in films. What I didn't realise was that they also carry water which they empty out of the balloon for the same reason.

You can imagine that there's very little protection from the weather when you're up there in a balloon. But it's not all bad. Large balloons have a curtain that they can pull round the basket to stop the rain coming in. They can leak, but at least they keep the worst of the rain out.

The second day of the festival, I got up before breakfast to go and watch 500 balloons take off. It takes your breath away to watch the sunrise as they lift off into the sky. My new ambition now is to go for a trip in a hot-air balloon! I can hardly wait!

[pause]

Now you will hear Part Two again.

tone

[The recording is repeated.]

[pause]

That is the end of Part Two.

Now turn to Part Three.

[pause]

PART 3

You will hear five short extracts in which students are talking about starting at university. For questions 19 to 23, choose from the list (A to H) what each speaker says about how they felt. Use the letters only once. There are three extra letters which you do not need to use.

You now have thirty seconds to look at Part Three.

[pause]

tone

Speaker 1

On my first day at university, there were a few things I did feel quite concerned about, like whether or not the other students would be the kind of people I'd get on with. But I had great faith in the fact that the course would be what I'd signed up for. And that's been the case. The work's been challenging and stimulating, and naturally there have been times when I haven't been able to follow a lecturer's argument, which is frustrating. But getting on top of things like that is what university study is all about.

[pause]

Speaker 2

The first day, there weren't any lectures, the focus was on getting to know the other people you'd be studying with for the next few years. Although I could see the point of that, what I really wanted to do was get on with lectures, essays, and things. After all, I thought, that's why I was there, wasn't I? Now I'm actually glad we were given the opportunity to socialise right at the beginning. I made loads of new friends! And I needn't have worried – there's been plenty of work to do since then. In fact, I sometimes struggle to fit it all in.

[pause]

Speaker 3

At school, I'd always had a close group of friends, and we'd meet to do our homework together. I felt I needed similar support at university as I didn't feel confident in my academic ability. On my first day, I wondered whether I'd meet enough new people who were also interested in working hard, and that turned out to be the case, fortunately. A couple of my school friends were doing the same course at another university, and they encouraged me from the very beginning, telling me to believe in myself and stop thinking I wouldn't be able to cope with all the essays and so on. And sure enough, I'm finding it fine.

[pause]

Speaker 4

We had lectures from the very first day – we were given maps of the university, a timetable, and basically told to get on with it. I didn't find it as hard finding my way around the campus as I did having to make new friends. I kept wishing I was back with my classmates I grew up with. It took a little time for me to settle in because of that, but the first day was the worst. Luckily I'm over it, and there are so many students here that I've found plenty of people I really get on with. But I remember that first day – it was hard.

[pause]

Speaker 5

[pause]

I'd expected there to be loads of students on my particular course, but there weren't. That was a let-down, really, but the feeling didn't last long because I went on to meet plenty of interesting people who were studying other subjects. Eventually, they became really good friends … just as close as those I'd made at school. Of course I also got to know loads of interesting people doing other courses – it was a real buzz, going from a small school in the countryside to a city university like I did. I really felt the world was opening up for me.

[pause]

Now you will hear Part Three again.

tone

[The recording is repeated.]

[pause]

That is the end of Part Three.

Now turn to Part Four.

[pause]

PART 4 *You will hear part of an interview with a marine biologist called Ed Shapiro, who is talking about a diving project in the Pitcairn Islands in the South Pacific. For questions 24 to 30, choose the best answer (A, B or C).*

You now have one minute to look at Part Four.

[pause]

tone

Interviewer: I'm in one of the most remote places in the world, the Pitcairn Islands in the South Pacific, with marine biologist, Ed Shapiro. Ed, tell us what you're doing here.

Ed: Hi. We're carrying out a survey of the marine environment around the islands, exploring the coral reef on the southern end of one at present. The reef here is unlike any we've come across in terms of varieties and sizes of the organisms. Compared to some areas, it's virtually unspoilt – so our aim is to obtain an idea of what oceans were like before the impacts of global warming and increased levels of CO_2. In years to come, however, this area too will become exposed to these things, unless something is done.

Interviewer: Have you been diving today?

Ed: I dive every day for at least two hours, in the morning and afternoon. This morning's dive was fairly standard. I was down there for a couple of hours, carrying on with my work documenting the living things I saw on the reef … how they interact with each other in this particular ecological environment. I take photographs as well as recording and logging what I've seen once I'm back on deck.

Interviewer: Is photography essential in order to record marine life?

Ed: Yes – I'm learning how to use underwater cameras more effectively. They capture things words can't, though people are completely used to astonishing pictures nowadays. Cameras are one of our tools, not just for documentation but also for getting our message across to the public. But we're always looking for new ways to do this – and it takes more than photos to wake people up …

Interviewer: Do you ever get frightened diving?

Ed: Every diver's fear is being lost at sea, which could happen if there's a sudden change in conditions. There's a strict set of safety procedures – we carry a flashlight, plus a special instrument that sends out a signal. I was pretty glad I had that to connect with my colleagues the other day. The waters were choppy, and the strong currents had me drifting – very scary at the depth I was at. People think sharks are the scariest thing in the sea, but they don't represent much of a threat … they're a common sight.

Interviewer: So tell us about how your career developed.

Ed: Marine biology's a competitive field, and the pay isn't necessarily great. If you're thinking of becoming a marine biologist, you have to accept there's a good chance that you may not find exactly the job you want. A degree and then a doctorate are the classic route – also, get involved with conservation organisations – all of which I did, happily. Then you could find yourself invited on an exciting expedition like this one! I was passionate about the sea as a child. The younger you start diving, the better.

Interviewer: How do you feel being 14,000 kilometres from home? Is homesickness a problem?

Ed: It could be, but the whole boat crew and I get along pretty well! There are some great people and we're all caught up in the day-to-day stuff, trying to maximise the benefits of our time here, an experience we may never get again. We don't have time to stay in touch with people back home – we don't forget about them, but time passes quickly. Obviously we do have the occasional dull moment, but there's always something on the boat that needs our attention.

Interviewer: It's an amazing place. You're obviously happy in your work, Ed.

Ed: Absolutely. The clarity of the waters around these reefs means fish thrive and we've recorded several new types for the first time – always a highlight in this profession. Several journalists have reported our findings, so that means the story of this marine world's getting out there. We've done surveys of deeper habitats by dropping cameras down to 1,600 metres, revealing some really unusual creatures. Most action, though, is between ten to twenty metres down, where the vast majority of marine life co-exists together on the reef …

[pause]

Now you will hear Part Four again.

tone

[The recording is repeated.]

[pause]

That is the end of Part Four.

There will now be a pause of five minutes for you to copy your answers onto the separate answer sheet. Be sure to follow the numbering of all the questions. I shall remind you when there is one minute left, so that you are sure to finish in time.

[pause – four minutes]

You have one more minute left.

[pause – one minute]

That is the end of the test. Please stop now. Your supervisor will now collect all the question papers and answer sheets.

Test 3 answer key

Reading and Use of English

Answer key with extra explanations in Resource bank

Part 1

1 C **2** A **3** C **4** C **5** B **6** A **7** D **8** B

Part 2

9 it/this **10** who/that **11** myself **12** by/past/away
13 front **14** on **15** Although/While/Whilst **16** anywhere

Part 3

17 intention(s) **18** evident **19** weight **20** fortunate
21 foundation(s) **22** straighten **23** restoration **24** confidently

Part 4

25 to GIVE her | a ring/call
26 MIGHT be/get/feel offended / take offence | if
27 was not/wasn't ALLOWED | to
28 MANAGED to win | on their
29 had/spent | more TIME
30 will/'ll be | an INCREASE in

Part 5

31 D **32** C **33** C **34** B **35** A **36** D

Part 6

37 D **38** F **39** A **40** G **41** E **42** B

Part 7

43 A **44** C **45** B **46** D **47** C **48** A **49** D
50 B **51** C **52** A

Listening

Answer key with extra explanations in Resource bank

Part 1

1 A **2** C **3** C **4** B **5** A **6** A **7** C **8** B

Part 2

9 exhibition **10** camper/camping van **11** morning
12 parachute jump **13** diamond ring **14** small island
15 fuel/gas/petrol **16** mosquito net **17** poem **18** tent

Part 3

19 G **20** C **21** B **22** H **23** A

Part 4

24 A **25** C **26** B **27** A **28** B **29** B **30** B

Audioscript

Test Three.

I am going to give you the instructions for this test. I shall introduce each part of the test and give you time to look at the questions. At the start of each piece you will hear this sound:

tone

You will hear each piece twice.

Remember, while you are listening, write your answers on the question paper. You will have five minutes at the end of the test to copy your answers onto the separate answer sheet.

There will now be a pause. Please ask any questions now, because you must not speak during the test.

[pause]

Now open your question paper and look at Part One.

[pause]

PART 1 *You will hear people talking in eight different situations. For questions 1 to 8, choose the best answer (A, B or C).*

Question 1 *You hear a man talking to a friend about a bicycle shop.*

[pause]

tone

Man: The bike shop I use is in Green Street, next to quite a nice café. Do you remember I told you about it? People often go there and have a coffee and a piece of cake while they're having their bike fixed – I know you'd like that!

Woman: Yes, I would!

Man: Anyway, if you ever need to go after work, it isn't far from here. They have a good range of cycling equipment and the staff are very helpful. They also have maps of the local area, with all the best routes for cyclists.

Woman: OK, thanks. I do need to check a couple of things on my bike ...

[pause]

tone

[The recording is repeated.]

[pause]

Question 2 *You hear a TV producer talking about reality programmes on TV.*

[pause]

tone

Woman: Some of these reality programmes have enormous viewing figures – they're incredibly popular at the time. But there's a massive difference between the popularity of a game show or a reality show and something that's really going to stand the test of time – to leave a legacy. Don't get me wrong – reality shows entertain and they're well-made, but quality drama series are in a different class. Viewers will be watching those re-runs in fifty years' time, unlike the reality shows. You've got to look at the long game. It's a marathon, not a sprint.

[pause]

tone

[The recording is repeated.]

[pause]

Question 3 *You hear two writers talking about writing dialogue.*

[pause]

tone

Man: You have a wonderful ear for natural-sounding dialogue in your novels. Where does that come from? Do you deliberately listen to other people's conversations?

Woman: I don't consciously do that. But I think writing dialogue is like being able to draw. Some people can, some people can't. Spoken language is quite different from written language, so as a writer, it's a very difficult thing to master … how to write down the language of speech so that it rings true.

Man: It certainly is interesting that so few writers can produce great dialogue instinctively.

[pause]

tone

[The recording is repeated.]

[pause]

Question 4 *You hear a woman telling a friend about a long train journey she's been on.*

[pause]

tone

Woman: I really enjoyed that long train journey I did.

Man: Really? I'd be bored having to sit there and do nothing for eight hours!

Woman: I didn't mind – I mean you have to make sure you get up and walk around from time to time, because there isn't too much leg room – especially if you're sitting by the window with another passenger next to you, like I was. But what I liked about my seat was the fact that I could relax and think about nothing, and really have time to appreciate all the stunning views. I did try to talk to the woman sitting next to me from time to time, but she mainly wanted to sleep.

[pause]

tone

[The recording is repeated.]

[pause]

Question 5 *You hear a man telling a friend about a holiday he's recently been on.*

[pause]

tone

Woman: Hi Kevin, how was your holiday?

Man: Very relaxing, thanks.

Woman: Did you book everything online?

Man: No, only the flights. I went to my local travel agent and they recommended the hotel. I couldn't have found a better deal myself.

Woman: Was there plenty to see?

Man: I suppose I'd have been to more places if I'd taken a good guidebook – but I didn't feel the need to see everything there was to see.

Woman: I know what you mean ... So, where are the photos?

Man: I can show you some now – though unusually for me, there aren't that many. I missed an opportunity there. Anyway, it was great fun.

[pause]

tone

[The recording is repeated.]

[pause]

Question 6 *You hear a woman talking on the radio about the arts.*

[pause]

tone

Woman: It's always been one of my favourite books and I've read it so many times that I've got a really clear picture of what the characters are like and so on. So when I heard they were adapting it for TV, I was a bit anxious, and decided I wouldn't watch it in case it spoilt the book for me. Then I heard that money had been raised to adapt it for the big screen and the author had written the screenplay. I watched it with my friend, who's also a fan, and we loved it – along with the rest of the audience.

[pause]

tone

[The recording is repeated.]

[pause]

Question 7 *You hear two students discussing their college.*

[pause]

tone

Girl: Hi Lucas, how's it going?

Boy: OK, thanks – though I guess it always takes a little while to get used to a new place.

Girl: Yeah, I was surprised at the condition of some of the teaching rooms. Bigger windows and a fresh coat of paint would make a huge difference.

Boy: Hmm, I agree. And I've found it less than easy to actually get hold of some of the staff outside class times, which doesn't reflect well on them. But the football and hockey fields are well-looked after – that isn't the case at a lot of colleges.

Girl: I must say all my teachers are really approachable and have given me plenty of good advice, and also the gym's very well equipped, so I'm not complaining.

[pause]

tone

[The recording is repeated.]

[pause]

Question 8 *You hear a child psychologist talking about the impact of noise on very young children.*

[pause]

tone

Man: Recent data from our laboratory suggests that very young children can recognise speech but only when the environment is relatively quiet. If we as adults find a situation too noisy, we can do something about it, we can turn down the TV or radio, or move to a quieter room. Babies can't do that. They depend on us to do it for them. But we're only likely to do this if the noise level is difficult for us too. We need to be much more aware of the impact that this noise might have on children, and make a point of reducing it when we are interacting with our children.

[pause]

tone

[The recording is repeated.]

[pause]

That is the end of Part One.

Now turn to Part Two.

[pause]

PART 2

You will hear a woman called Jane Hughes talking about total solar eclipses, which happen when the Moon comes between the Sun and the Earth and blocks out the light from the Sun. For questions 9 to 18, complete the sentences with a word or short phrase.

You now have forty-five seconds to look at Part Two.

[pause]

tone

Hello, my name's Jane Hughes and I, like a number of people around the world, am fascinated by total solar eclipses. That's when the Moon moves between the Sun and the Earth and blocks out the light from the Sun for a short time. For years, I took absolutely no interest in eclipses, and tended to skip any article on the subject I saw in the newspaper. It wasn't until I was taken to an exhibition that was absolutely fascinating and turned out to be all about them that I realised I'd actually like to witness one for myself.

A total solar eclipse happens approximately every 18 months, somewhere on Earth. And in order to see the full effect, you have to be in a particular place at a particular time. In the case of the first eclipse I went to watch, that place was in Australia. I took the cheapest flight I could find from London to Sydney, and then a train to a small town several hundred kilometres away. I rented a camper van to reach the spot where some other eclipse chasers, as people like me are commonly known, were gathering.

Eclipses can happen at any time during daylight hours, and this one took place first thing in the morning. I'll never forget it. It can feel very strange when it suddenly goes dark at one o'clock on a sunny summer's afternoon.

I felt a huge rush of emotion ... I've had some memorable experiences in my life, like going on a night dive in Madagascar or finally managing to run a half marathon, but when it went dark, for two long minutes, the closest this came to for me – in terms of sheer excitement – was when I once did a parachute jump. But don't just take my word for it, go out and try it for yourselves if you ever get the opportunity.

And just before the total eclipse, as well as just as it ends, there's a tiny flash of brilliant light which astronomers call the 'diamond ring' effect. We were just amazed and stood in complete silence.

So then I was hooked, and started planning how to see my next eclipse as soon as I got home. That one, my second, would prove to be even more of a challenge to watch. To get as much as three minutes of darkness during this total eclipse, the ideal location would be surrounded by open ocean – a small island – because seen from the nearest large land mass, the eclipse would be far shorter.

However, that was easier said than done. A group of us had to travel for about six hours in a little boat, carrying all the food and water we'd need on board. However, the boat we'd hired had no fuel, and until the captain managed to find some, we thought we might not be able to reach our destination.

It was an exciting trip across some quite rough water, and when we got there, I spread my sleeping bag on the sand. I was very grateful for the mosquito net I'd packed too, which I attached to a tree branch above my head. We went straight to sleep under the stars.

Once again, it was completely magical. Of course, I realise not everyone can do this, or would want to. You can look online for great photographs of eclipses, as well as video clips and articles explaining the phenomenon. You might even come across a poem I wrote, my attempt to describe how it feels to witness these events.

I'm already dreaming about my next trip. I must buy a tent to take with me – the one I have is far too heavy. I have special glasses so I can watch eclipses without damaging my eyes, and a solar filter for camera lenses is essential. That's all the special equipment I need.

So, if you'd like to ask anything …

[pause]

Now you will hear Part Two again.

tone

[The recording is repeated.]

[pause]

That is the end of Part Two.

Now turn to Part Three.

[pause]

PART 3

You will hear five short extracts in which people are talking about walking to work. For questions 19 to 23, choose from the list (A to H) how each speaker says they benefit from walking to work. Use the letters only once. There are three extra letters which you do not need to use.

You now have thirty seconds to look at Part Three.

[pause]

tone

Speaker 1

Walking any distance is usually a planned leisure activity or some sort of health aid – to help people lose weight or keep fit. But there's something else people get from choosing to walk – it's a space to think. After I'd opted to walk to work instead of taking the bus, I began to sense a sort of empathy and togetherness with the many workers who were doing the same thing every morning. And that's never gone away. I arrive at work in a more laid-back frame of mind, and colleagues say I seem much calmer.

[pause]

Speaker 2

There's a lot to look at. I'm always spotting strange little streets, interesting cafés, things I wouldn't have paid attention to if I'd driven or taken public transport. I'm lucky the distance between my home and office isn't that great, but there's enough variety to offer opportunities for a little urban exploration, and I can allow myself a certain flexibility, which is good. If I'm a bit stressed I'll make sure I pass through a park or somewhere with some wildlife. It's amazing how a relatively small change to my routine has brought so many improvements to my life.

[pause]

Speaker 3

A lot of people see walking from place to place as time lost from their busy schedules. I used to feel like that and be entirely focused on work, which wasn't great. But in fact, building that extra time into my morning for walking to the office has actually allowed me to take in what's around me, and gives me time. I've found myself thinking about everything I've got and how fortunate I am. It's just as well that I've always eaten a big breakfast before I set off for work … and of course the exercise does me good.

[pause]

Speaker 4

Although none of my colleagues have commented on the difference in how I look, I've been pleased with the change. I got fed up going to the gym in an effort to lose weight and build some muscles – I just couldn't face it after a day at my desk, so I switched to walking to work. And now I never feel bad about walking even when it's a bit chilly. And whereas once I would've jumped on a bus, which would've been quicker, now I just enjoy the fresh air.

[pause]

Speaker 5

I've been walking to work for months – I must know every road there is in the area between my flat and my office. Walking requires a certain amount of attention, but it leaves enough of the time open to thinking. I reckon once you get the blood flowing through the brain it starts working faster and more creatively. It means <u>by the time I get to the office I can really focus on a task and get things done</u>. I used to be like my colleagues – drinking coffee and feeling sleepy. I find I have brighter eyes and clearer skin too, despite all the invisible pollution in cities.

[pause]

Now you will hear Part Three again.

tone

[The recording is repeated.]

[pause]

That is the end of Part Three.

Now turn to Part Four.

[pause]

PART 4 *You will hear an interview with a woman called Sarah Featherstone, who runs a website called Coffee Lovers. For questions 24 to 30, choose the best answer (A, B or C).*

You now have one minute to look at Part Four.

[pause]

tone

Interviewer: Welcome to the programme, Sarah. What gave you the idea for starting a website on coffee shops in the UK?

Sarah: Well, in most other European countries there's a well-established coffee culture, but here in Britain it started considerably later. There was a time when tourists had to search far and wide for a decent cup of coffee. In recent years we've had a number of big international companies come in and put identical coffee shops in every city centre, but my website is about the small, independent, coffee shops. Their product is generally far superior, in my view, and they often struggle against the financial might of these big internationals, so I suppose I wanted to promote them.

Interviewer: Now, tell us a bit about your coffee website.

Sarah: Well in its current form, users are directed to a menu of different towns – that's a new development. Clicking on the one you want brings up a webpage for each recommended coffee shop, where you can find a written review by us, tons of photos, a map, and a link to a customer review page which is starting to grow. And it's all paid for by external advertising … not by the coffee shops! Obviously if coffee shops were allowed to advertise, that would be against the spirit of the website, as it's meant to be unbiased opinion, not somewhere for the shops to publicise themselves.

Interviewer: So I imagine you must reject some of the coffee shops you visit?

Sarah: Yes … two out of every three, usually, don't make it onto the site. Last week we rejected a place where the seating and décor just weren't welcoming. With most places the coffee itself is good … it's rare for it to be bad enough to put us off. More often it would be the attitude of the staff that didn't please us for one reason or another when we visited.

Interviewer: So what did you write about the coffee shop we're in now, the Old Mill House?

Sarah: Well we like very small coffee shops that have real character, and also an unusual and unique selling point for the public. The Old Mill House have always been great at this. It used to be their colourful plants and interesting paintings, but other shops soon copied them. Now it's the humorous messages they put up on their chalk boards – things like special offers, requests to visitors, and so on. Other places in the city have fantastic, unique ideas too – such as board games for customers to play.

Interviewer: And we're going next to one called the Pink Peacock?

Sarah: Yes, at the Peacock they've really set out to make the accompanying food their speciality. Their pies are nothing short of amazing, although they are a bit pricey. But what strikes you with a place so small is that they seem to be able to cater for every request: gluten-free cakes, wheat-free bread, lactose-free milk. And they appear to do an excellent takeaway trade, so they're clearly very well organised and well supplied.

Interviewer: So Sarah ... tell me a bit about why you set up your own business.

Sarah: Well, after leaving college I got through quite a few part-time jobs, including a couple as a waitress. Then I worked as an administrator in a law firm … I was there for ten years until unfortunately I was made redundant. I decided to use my redundancy money to set up a business, and after a lot of research … and I guess thinking back to my earlier waitressing days … I thought about opening a coffee shop. Well, doing that seemed an easy way of losing all my money if I got it wrong, but the website … that idea seemed a better path to follow.

Interviewer: And what plans do you have for your website in the future?

Sarah: Well, it's important to keep moving with it. The obvious thing is to start covering coffee shops abroad and to see whether that's popular. To limit it I might just start off with capital cities in Europe. Longer-term I do intend to look into the possibility of an app which would alert people to the nearest good coffee shop. Also some kind of rating system like using stars is something I've been considering for ages … although with that idea I don't want to be seen to be copying other similar websites.

[pause]

Now you will hear Part Four again.

tone

[The recording is repeated.]

[pause]

That is the end of Part Four.

There will now be a pause of five minutes for you to copy your answers onto the separate answer sheet. Be sure to follow the numbering of all the questions. I shall remind you when there is one minute left, so that you are sure to finish in time.

[pause – four minutes]

You have one more minute left.

[pause – one minute]

That is the end of the test. Please stop now. Your supervisor will now collect all the question papers and answer sheets.

Test 4 answer key

Reading and Use of English

Answer key with extra explanations in Resource bank

Part 1

1 C **2** B **3** D **4** B **5** A **6** D **7** B **8** C

Part 2

9 for **10** up **11** to **12** or **13** are
14 what **15** it **16** another

Part 3

17 success **18** psychological **19** tension **20** frightening
21 appearance **22** distraction **23** exaggeration **24** truth

Part 4

25 to be EMPLOYED | in/by/at
26 NEVER stopped | raining
27 it('s/is) DIFFICULT | to understand
28 an INCREASE | in
29 in NEED | of
30 to pay/give (more) | ATTENTION to

Part 5

31 A **32** B **33** C **34** D **35** B **36** A

Part 6

37 D **38** F **39** A **40** G **41** B **42** E

Part 7

43 E **44** B **45** A **46** D **47** B **48** C **49** B **50** A **51** C **52** A

Listening

Answer key with extra explanations in Resource bank

Part 1

1 B **2** A **3** A **4** C **5** A **6** B **7** A **8** B

Part 2

9 research assistant/researcher **10** cleaning (up)
11 heavy metal **12** 35,000/thirty-five thousand
13 diversity **14** (live) poetry **15** inspiration
16 network **17** agents **18** admin(istration)/administrative

Part 3

19 E **20** C **21** G **22** D **23** B

Part 4

24 C **25** A **26** A **27** C **28** C **29** C **30** B

Audioscript

Test Four.

I am going to give you the instructions for this test. I shall introduce each part of the test and give you time to look at the questions. At the start of each piece you will hear this sound:

tone

You will hear each piece twice.

Remember, while you are listening, write your answers on the question paper. You will have five minutes at the end of the test to copy your answers onto the separate answer sheet.

There will now be a pause. Please ask any questions now, because you must not speak during the test.

[pause]

Now open your question paper and look at Part One.

[pause]

PART 1 *You will hear people talking in eight different situations. For questions 1 to 8, choose the best answer (A, B or C).*

Question 1 *You hear an actress talking about her new part in a play.*

[pause]

tone

Woman: I think it's a great show, which gives the audience a fantastic night out. There are plenty of laughs, but there are also moments when the audience will gasp at what they see. It's such a great part for a woman of my age and there aren't many of those about. My character, the mother, finds her loyalties divided within the family. It's powerful stuff and that's why I jumped at the chance of playing her. The male lead is played by Sam Yates. I've worked closely with him before on TV, but it'll be fun for both of us to see if we can re-create the chemistry between us on stage.

[pause]

tone

[The recording is repeated.]

[pause]

Question 2 *You hear two friends talking about a restaurant.*

[pause]

tone

Woman: Well, they've really changed that place, haven't they? The first time we went, it was like going back in time – and not in a good way!

Man: And the menu wasn't very inspiring then either. I was surprised when you suggested going there again actually.

Woman: Well, I heard it was under new management and had improved, and I just wanted to see what they'd done. It certainly seems to be working. There were people waiting for tables this time and the staff could hardly keep up. They were rushed off their feet.

Man: I felt sorry for them. They need to take on more people.

[pause]

tone

[The recording is repeated.]

[pause]

Question 3 *You hear two students talking about a visit to a museum.*

[pause]

tone

Woman: I must say I don't always enjoy tours of museum galleries, but I thought the guide was really good, didn't you?

Man: Well yeah, I mean luckily ancient Egypt is a fascinating topic, so he already had our interest before he even opened his mouth. But I agree he was great, and clearly <u>very familiar with all the objects in the gallery</u> – he could probably have spent the whole time talking about just one or two of them.

Woman: I'm glad he didn't though!

Man: I know – there were so many different things to see – but it would've been good to have the chance to ask more questions, wouldn't it?

Woman: Yes, you're right.

[pause]

tone

[The recording is repeated.]

[pause]

Question 4 *You hear talk given by a child psychologist.*

[pause]

tone

Woman: Parental restrictions on outdoor play have considerable consequences for children's health and future well-being. <u>Kids should have space to explore and run around.</u> Also, playing in the dirt seems to strengthen the immune system; in other words, it stimulates the body's defences. If you restrict outdoor play, you also restrict stimulation of the immune system. The system then responds inappropriately to stimuli, and that probably explains the rise in allergies such as asthma. <u>Without free outdoor play, kids lack the ability to get together and play spontaneously. Playing freely with others lets kids develop their social skills</u>, and when free play is denied, so are those opportunities.

[pause]

tone

[The recording is repeated.]

[pause]

Question 5	*You hear part of a radio phone-in discussion about a proposal to redevelop one part of a city.*
	[pause]
	tone
Woman:	We're discussing the recently announced proposal to demolish the old athletics stadium in the city and build three new apartment blocks on the site. Our next caller is Dennis.
Man:	Hi. A couple of questions came to me about this proposal. How many people from the area could really afford a flat in the kind of buildings the developers have in mind? And, while it might seem ridiculous to question the idea of creating a green space planted with trees around the site, would young people be able to use it for sports and other activities or would it be intended – as seems likely – for the occupants of the new luxury blocks?
	[pause]
	tone
	[The recording is repeated.]
	[pause]
Question 6	*You hear two people talking on the radio about an exhibition of work by a wildlife photographer.*
	[pause]
	tone
Man:	I expected the photos to be of animals in the wild rather than with all the natural background taken out. It made for a powerful effect without the details that a lot of photographers tend to be interested in.
Woman:	They were all shot in that style so you focused on the animals themselves. I guess that was his intention as a photographer – to force you to observe their faces.
Man:	There's little doubt about that. He's trying to draw attention to sadness at the loss of their natural environment. Quite depressing. Those ones of the gorillas all had that same effect on me.
Man:	Avoiding the standard settings for wildlife shots had stunning results.
	[pause]
	tone
	[The recording is repeated.]
	[pause]

Question 7 — *You hear a man telling a colleague about a workshop he will attend.*

[pause]

tone

Woman: So you're off to that workshop, I see.

Man: I think the workshop is going to be quite hard work actually. You're allowed to attend on condition that you've done some preparation for it. I've read a few articles by the main presenters – just because I was interested – it wasn't a requirement. <u>And I've heard a series of podcasts. They sent us a link to those in the pre-course information email. We need to do that beforehand so we get the best out of the day.</u> During the workshop we're encouraged to take notes and raise any issues that concern us, but we can't film or take photos.

[pause]

tone

[The recording is repeated.]

[pause]

Question 8 — *You hear two friends talking about the football team they support.*

[pause]

tone

Woman: So, we won again last night.

Man: Yeah, I watched it on TV. I've seen many more entertaining matches than that, but at least we didn't lose.

Woman: Apparently, the manager had another row with some newspaper reporters. They asked him why he hadn't selected certain players for the match, and he said it was none of their business. He was quite rude, I think.

Man: Well, it gives reporters something to write about, so I doubt if they're bothered really. <u>The fact is, though, that the team haven't been at all exciting to watch recently, and that's the manager's responsibility.</u> He isn't interested in exciting footballers – winning's everything for him, which is a pity.

[pause]

tone

[The recording is repeated.]

[pause]

That is the end of Part One.

Now turn to Part Two.

[pause]

PART 2

You will hear a man called Victor Medway talking to some students about his job, helping to organise a music festival. For questions 9 to 18, complete the sentences with a word or short phrase.

You now have forty-five seconds to look at Part Two.

[pause]

tone

Hello. My name's Victor Medway and I'm responsible for planning and organising music festivals.

So, how did I come to be in this line of work? I've actually had a passion for music since my early teens, and my dream was to be a DJ on the radio. Alternatively, I wanted to be the producer of radio programmes. I never managed to land that kind of job, but I did end up as a research assistant on radio shows. I enjoyed that for a while and it gave me some useful experience.

But after a couple of years I wanted to try something different and my friend suggested volunteering at a music festival. In exchange for free entry to the festival, you work for a few hours each day. For example, a volunteer might help out by providing first aid or handing out bottles of water. I started by cleaning up during a festival. After four days of that, I decided I'd try and get a paid job with a music festival, and I got lucky.

So just to give you an idea of what my job is like, at the moment I'm booking the acts for a summer festival called Wavelength. This year, we'll have about eighty acts in total. We'll be opening with Antimatter, the electronic dance music act, while the final-day headliners are the rock legends, Ghost. Earlier this week, I managed to persuade a world-famous heavy metal band – I'm not allowed to name them yet – to appear on day two.

The first Wavelength festival took place ten years ago, and it's grown enormously since then. In the first year, about 5,000 people turned up. Now, based on ticket applications, we reckon we could attract around 75,000 over the four days, although the size of the venue restricts us to 35,000. Tickets for this year are sold out, by the way.

Wavelength has changed in other ways over the years. The facilities are better than they were, and the whole operation is run with greater efficiency. In the past, Wavelength was often accused of not having enough diversity – too many acts looked and sounded the same. We still get comments like that but there's nothing really to justify them now. This year's line-up has music to suit all tastes.

Also, while music is still the main focus of Wavelength, with four different stages for it, we do cater for other interests. We have a large tent for comedy acts each year, and this time round we've got people performing live poetry – something we've never had before. We even have a tent where circus performers entertain festival-goers.

I spend lots of time keeping track of the music scene globally. It's important to have the latest information about things like album releases and bands' touring schedules. I also go to music festivals around the world, mainly because of the inspiration I get there – seeing different ways of presenting music, for example, or certain musicians who I might end up booking for Wavelength.

Of course, every organiser wants their own festival to get the best acts and the biggest crowds, so there's competition between them. When it comes to festivals with similar musical profiles, there's often a particular rivalry. But I actually talk a lot to other festival organisers and over time a network has formed, which has been very useful for sharing information and advice.

I have contact with other music industry people too. Musicians themselves can be unpredictable, but once you get to know them, they're usually fine. Their agents – the people you make bookings with – are often quite awkward to deal with. You'd think they'd jump at the publicity that festival appearances can give their clients. Musicians' managers are often demanding too, but you can understand why – their role is to protect their acts.

To succeed as a festival organiser, you need to be persuasive, and, fortunately, I have pretty effective communication skills – something I was born with, I guess. It's also important to be good at administration, and I've had to make a big effort to achieve that. A love of music definitely helps too, though you don't have to be a musician – my musical skills are very limited.

[pause]

Now you will hear Part Two again.

tone

[The recording is repeated.]

[pause]

That is the end of Part Two.

Now turn to Part Three.

[pause]

PART 3

You will hear five short extracts in which people are talking about a cookery course they participated in. For questions 19 to 23, choose from the list (A to H) what each speaker liked best about the course. Use the letters only once. There are three extra letters which you do not need to use.

You now have thirty seconds to look at Part Three.

[pause]

tone

Speaker 1

My mother paid for me and my sister to do a cake-making course. Our class had the teacher's undivided and expert attention, along with her two assistants, for the morning, making four cakes using the traditional ingredients. The teacher really knew her stuff. When it came to baking, I got to grips with some really clever tricks of the trade, and that was really valuable for me. We'd tried making the same cakes before – although they'd never worked out, but under her expert guidance, we managed to produce some very professional-looking cakes. They even tasted good too! My Mom was very impressed. She thought we'd popped into a shop on the way home and bought them!

[pause]

Speaker 2

The chef, Stefan, was very enthusiastic and had a great sense of humour, which is very important when you have such a diverse group of students. The kitchen was well equipped, although the two cookers were pretty ancient, and we had to provide our own ingredients. We all got to decide what dish we wanted to cook, and there were some very interesting ideas. In the end, mine seemed to be the one everyone wanted to taste. The high spot of the course, though, was just spending time with my fellow students – sitting down around a big table and chatting about our dishes.

[pause]

Speaker 3

I'm a vegetarian and I booked a course on vegetarian cooking as a way of increasing the range of recipes I can prepare. The day was extremely well organised. Our instructor John was incredibly knowledgeable and if you wanted advice about anything, he would willingly give it to you. There were only six students, which meant we all got plenty of help and all got involved in each other's cooking experience … although some people didn't know when to hold back. I now have exactly what I wanted – a variety of dishes that allows me to meet my own dietary needs as well as keep a hungry family satisfied. What more could you want?

[pause]

Speaker 4

The class was limited to 12 students, with plenty of preparation space for each person. Each day we were given a set of recipes, each revolving around a theme. There was, quite rightly, a real emphasis on sourcing good quality produce straight from the fields, which I particularly appreciated. You could certainly taste the difference in the finished dish! The teacher was always available when you needed her. I really felt I was in good hands. If you got stuck on some of the more technical bits, she was always more than happy to fully explain the problem, addressing the entire class, so we really learnt as a group.

[pause]

Speaker 5

[pause]

As a parent, I'm always looking for activities that will stimulate and educate my children rather than simply entertain them, so I signed us all up for a cookery course. The kids really enjoyed experimenting with chocolate recipes – they came up with some crazy ideas for dishes, but what really made it for me was getting to use the state-of-the-art cooker. I could never have afforded anything like that at home. The challenge of making such delicious recipes really stretched us all, but when you're using the most up-to-date things available, everything seems much simpler. The teacher was so patient and really knew her stuff. I'd definitely take the kids on one of these again.

[pause]

Now you will hear Part Three again.

tone

[The recording is repeated.]

[pause]

That is the end of Part Three.

Now turn to Part Four.

[pause]

PART 4 *You will hear an interview with Terry Bankcroft, whose company, Get Running, organises overseas marathons, talking about his work. For questions 24 to 30, choose the best answer (A, B or C).*

You now have one minute to look at Part Four.

[pause]

tone

Interviewer: Terry, thank you for coming to speak to us today about your business called Get Running. Now, you organise marathons all over the world. How did you get into running in the first place?

Terry: Well, I had a successful career sitting in front of a computer, creating websites and designing apps. Then I met my wife and we discovered that we were both creative types who'd done a lot of running when we were younger. But as time went by, work and stuff had taken over. Jenny started running again about eight years ago. I didn't jump on the bandwagon straightaway, but I cheered her on from the side-lines! Her passion and energy were infectious and I took up running again.

Interviewer: Are you still as keen on running now as you were then?

Terry: Back then, when I started, it seemed like a lot of hard work and there's no denying it – it was painful! But as my endurance increased, I moved on from short distances and then I started competing. I don't think I'll ever stop – I can't imagine not doing it. It's led on to other things too. Now I mountain-bike, snowboard, ski – I'll try most things. I've become a more active all-round athlete.

Interviewer: Now, you organise international running events. What aspect do you find most challenging?

Terry: The planning is very time consuming. We spend months recruiting staff and volunteers, handling the advertising and promotion, and the logistics. Runners don't see all that and often query the cost of entry to the race. Having to explain that is the worst part for me. Another tricky bit is co-ordinating with government officials in the area. Cultural differences can cause misunderstandings, so I hand that part over to our local staff and I don't get involved.

Interviewer: You organise races in some interesting parts of the world. How do you choose the locations?

Terry: It's my own preference really. I've run all types of races and the ones I really remember are where I've gone off the beaten track and into nature. It's something magical to experience that. We chose our latest race site when we were on holiday in this amazing, lush region of China. I love taking the runners off the touristy path, into breathtakingly beautiful but remote locations.

Interviewer: You make good use of local volunteers to help run your races.

Terry: Yes, volunteers are the key to successful athletic events. It's a huge task to stage a race; the list of responsibilities we ask the volunteers to undertake is endless. In some respects, the runners are the stars of the show, but I make sure that the volunteers also get their moment in the spotlight too. Most of them are runners themselves, so they get a big kick out of helping out the competitors.

Interviewer: Now, tell me about the package tour side of what you do.

Terry: Yes, well, I organise the races, often with the assistance of a local partner organisation in the country concerned, but also I organise tours for the many runners who take part from overseas. They're responsible for their flights, but after that I take over … transporting them to and from the race site by coach.
I provide two nights' lodging, all meals and a separate sightseeing trip.

Interviewer: Now, on the running side, what advice would you give to a first-time runner in one of your events?

Terry: Well, don't get carried away in the excitement and go off too fast, only to run out of energy later. Also, just focus on your own running form and on giving your own best performance as well as you can. You can't control things like the weather, the other participants, possible injuries … anything can happen. You mustn't let thoughts of these things distract you.

[pause]

Now you will hear Part Four again.

tone

[The recording is repeated.]

[pause]

That is the end of Part Four.

There will now be a pause of five minutes for you to copy your answers onto the separate answer sheet. Be sure to follow the numbering of all the questions. I shall remind you when there is one minute left, so that you are sure to finish in time.

[pause – four minutes]

You have one more minute left.

[pause – one minute]

That is the end of the test. Please stop now. Your supervisor will now collect all the question papers and answer sheets.

38926

OFFICE USE ONLY - DO NOT WRITE OR MAKE ANY MARK ABOVE THIS LINE Page 1 of 2

Cambridge Assessment English

Candidate Name		Candidate Number	
Centre Name		Centre Number	
Examination Title		Examination Details	
Candidate Signature		Assessment Date	

Supervisor: If the candidate is ABSENT or has WITHDRAWN shade here ○

First Reading and Use of English Candidate Answer Sheet

Instructions

Use a PENCIL (B or HB).

Rub out any answer you want to change using an eraser.

Parts 1, 5, 6 and 7:
Mark ONE letter for each question.

For example, if you think A is the right answer to the question, mark your answer sheet like this: 0 A B C

Parts 2, 3 and 4: Write your answer clearly in CAPITAL LETTERS.

For parts 2 and 3, write one letter in each box. 0 EXAMPLE

Part 1

1	A ○	B ○	C ○	D ○
2	A ○	B ○	C ○	D ○
3	A ○	B ○	C ○	D ○
4	A ○	B ○	C ○	D ○
5	A ○	B ○	C ○	D ○
6	A ○	B ○	C ○	D ○
7	A ○	B ○	C ○	D ○
8	A ○	B ○	C ○	D ○

Part 2

		Do not write below here
9		9 1 ○ 0 ○
10		10 1 ○ 0 ○
11		11 1 ○ 0 ○
12		12 1 ○ 0 ○
13		13 1 ○ 0 ○
14		14 1 ○ 0 ○
15		15 1 ○ 0 ○
16		16 1 ○ 0 ○

Continues over →

OFFICE USE ONLY - DO NOT WRITE OR MAKE ANY MARK BELOW THIS LINE Page 1 of 2

38926

SAMPLE

© Cambridge Assessment 2020 Photocopiable

38926

OFFICE USE ONLY - DO NOT WRITE OR MAKE ANY MARK ABOVE THIS LINE

Part 3

Do not write below here

17		17 1 0
18		18 1 0
19		19 1 0
20		20 1 0
21		21 1 0
22		22 1 0
23		23 1 0
24		24 1 0

Part 4

Do not write below here

25		25 2 1 0
26		26 2 1 0
27		27 2 1 0
28		28 2 1 0
29		29 2 1 0
30		30 2 1 0

Part 5

31	A	B	C	D
32	A	B	C	D
33	A	B	C	D
34	A	B	C	D
35	A	B	C	D
36	A	B	C	D

Part 6

37	A	B	C	D	E	F	G
38	A	B	C	D	E	F	G
39	A	B	C	D	E	F	G
40	A	B	C	D	E	F	G
41	A	B	C	D	E	F	G
42	A	B	C	D	E	F	G

Part 7

43	A	B	C	D	E	F
44	A	B	C	D	E	F
45	A	B	C	D	E	F
46	A	B	C	D	E	F
47	A	B	C	D	E	F
48	A	B	C	D	E	F
49	A	B	C	D	E	F
50	A	B	C	D	E	F
51	A	B	C	D	E	F
52	A	B	C	D	E	F

OFFICE USE ONLY - DO NOT WRITE OR MAKE ANY MARK BELOW THIS LINE

Page 2 of 2

38926

SAMPLE

© Cambridge Assessment 2020 Photocopiable

20512

OFFICE USE ONLY - DO NOT WRITE OR MAKE ANY MARK ABOVE THIS LINE **Page 1 of 2**

Cambridge Assessment English

Candidate Name		**Candidate Number**	
Centre Name		**Centre Number**	
Examination Title		**Examination Details**	
Candidate Signature		**Assessment Date**	

Supervisor: If the candidate is ABSENT or has WITHDRAWN shade here ○

First Listening Candidate Answer Sheet

Instructions

Use a PENCIL (B or HB).

Rub out any answer you want to change using an eraser.

Parts 1, 3 and **4:**

Mark ONE letter for each question.

For example, if you think **A** is the right answer to the question, mark your answer sheet like this:

Part 2:

Write your answer clearly in CAPITAL LETTERS.

Write one letter or number in each box.
If the answer has more than one word, leave one box empty between words.

For example:

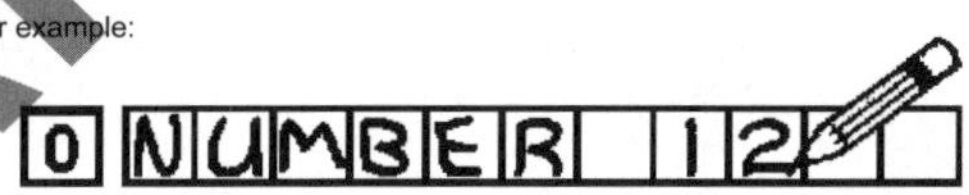

Turn this sheet over to start.

SAMPLE

OFFICE USE ONLY - DO NOT WRITE OR MAKE ANY MARK BELOW THIS LINE **Page 1 of 2**

20512

© Cambridge Assessment 2020 Photocopiable

20512

OFFICE USE ONLY - DO NOT WRITE OR MAKE ANY MARK ABOVE THIS LINE — Page 2 of 2

Part 1

1	A ○	B ○	C ○	5	A ○	B ○	C ○
2	A ○	B ○	C ○	6	A ○	B ○	C ○
3	A ○	B ○	C ○	7	A ○	B ○	C ○
4	A ○	B ○	C ○	8	A ○	B ○	C ○

Part 2 (Remember to write in CAPITAL LETTERS or numbers)

		Do not write below here
9		9 1 ○ 0 ○
10		10 1 ○ 0 ○
11		11 1 ○ 0 ○
12		12 1 ○ 0 ○
13		13 1 ○ 0 ○
14		14 1 ○ 0 ○
15		15 1 ○ 0 ○
16		16 1 ○ 0 ○
17		17 1 ○ 0 ○
18		18 1 ○ 0 ○

Part 3

19	A ○	B ○	C ○	D ○	E ○	F ○	G ○	H ○
20	A ○	B ○	C ○	D ○	E ○	F ○	G ○	H ○
21	A ○	B ○	C ○	D ○	E ○	F ○	G ○	H ○
22	A ○	B ○	C ○	D ○	E ○	F ○	G ○	H ○
23	A ○	B ○	C ○	D ○	E ○	F ○	G ○	H ○

Part 4

24	A ○	B ○	C ○
25	A ○	B ○	C ○
26	A ○	B ○	C ○
27	A ○	B ○	C ○
28	A ○	B ○	C ○
29	A ○	B ○	C ○
30	A ○	B ○	C ○

OFFICE USE ONLY - DO NOT WRITE OR MAKE ANY MARK BELOW THIS LINE — Page 2 of 2

20512

SAMPLE

© Cambridge Assessment 2020 Photocopiable

Part One Answer
You must write within the grey lines.

SAMPLE

© Cambridge Assessment 2020 Photocopiable

Part Two Answer You must write within the grey lines.	
Write your question number here:	

SAMPLE

© Cambridge Assessment 2020 Photocopiable

Acknowledgements

The authors and publishers acknowledge the following sources of copyright material and are grateful for the permissions granted. While every effort has been made, it has not always been possible to identify the sources of all the material used, or to trace all copyright holders. If any omissions are brought to our notice, we will be happy to include the appropriate acknowledgements on reprinting and in the next update to the digital edition, as applicable.

Key: S = Speaking, L = Listening, RUE = Reading and Use of English.

Text

L2: Balloon Fiesta for the text regarding hot air balloon festival. Reproduced with kind permission of Balloon Fiesta; **L4:** The Strong for the text excerpt from *The American Journal of Play (Volume 3, Issue 4 Spring 2011)*. Reproduced with permission of The Strong; Run Society Global for the excerpt from 'Marathon Organiser'. Copyright © 2011-2019 RunSociety Global. Reproduced with kind permission; **RUE1:** Little, Brown Book Group for the text from *RAFA: My Story* by Rafael Nadal and John Carlin. Copyright © 2012 Little, Brown Book Group. Reproduced with permission; Hachette Book Group for the text from *RAFA: My Story* by Rafael Nadal and John Carlin. Copyright © 2012 Hachette Book Group. Reproduced with permission of Hyperion, an imprint of Hachette Book Group, Inc.; Guardian News & Media Limited for the adapted text from 'Take video games seriously! Yes, they're fun, but they matter culturally too' by Naomi Alderman, *The Guardian* 2016. Copyright © Guardian News & Media Limited. Reproduced with permission; Bob Borson for the adapted text from 'Being an Architect' by Bob Borson. Copyright © Bob Borson. Reproduced with kind permission; **RUE2:** Houghton Mifflin Harcourt for the adapted text from *Africa in My Blood* by Jane Goodall and Dale Peterson. Copyright © 2001 Houghton Mifflin Harcourt. Reproduced with permission; Guardian News & Media Limited for the adapted text from 'The art of ebru: A colourful Turkish tradition finds a home in the UK' by Andrew Shields, *The Guardian* 2016. Copyright © Guardian News & Media Limited. Reproduced with permission; **RUE3:** Guardian News & Media Limited for the adapted text from "I've seen Les Misérables 1,027 times' … superfans of Star Wars, Madonna, Harry Potter and more' by Homa Khaleeli, *The Guardian* 2016. Copyright © Guardian News & Media Limited. Reproduced with permission; Guardian News & Media Limited for the text excerpt from 'How do I become a voiceover artist' by Anna Tims, copyright © 2013 Guardian News & Media Limited. Reproduced with permission; **RUE4:** Terry LaBan for the adapted text from 'So you want to be a cartoonist?' by Terry LaBan. Copyright © Terry LaBan. Reproduced with permission; Guardian News & Media Limited for the adapted text from 'A message in a bottle and a journey round the world' by Nione Meakin, *The Guardian* 2016. Copyright © Guardian News & Media Limited. Reproduced with permission; Richard Foster for the adapted text from 'What does a sports psychologist do? The man who works for Eddie Jones explains' by Richard Foster. Copyright © 2016 Richard Foster. Reproduced with permission.

Photography

All the photographs are sourced from Getty Images.

S1: vm/E+; Paul Bradbury/Caiaimage; raisbeckfoto/E+; Hero Images/DigitalVision; **S2:** Hero Images; vm/E+; Maskot; Jose Luis Pelaez Inc/DigitalVision; **S3:** Hero Images; Justin Pumfrey/Stone/Getty Images Plus; Hill Street Studios/DigitalVision; Flashpop/DigitalVision; **S4:** Klaus Vedfelt/DigitalVision; Hill Street Studios/DigitalVision; PeopleImages/E+; Fuse/Corbis.

Visual materials for the Speaking test

Why are the people using laptops in these places?

1A

1B

Why are the people learning about the natural world in these places?

1C

1D

1E

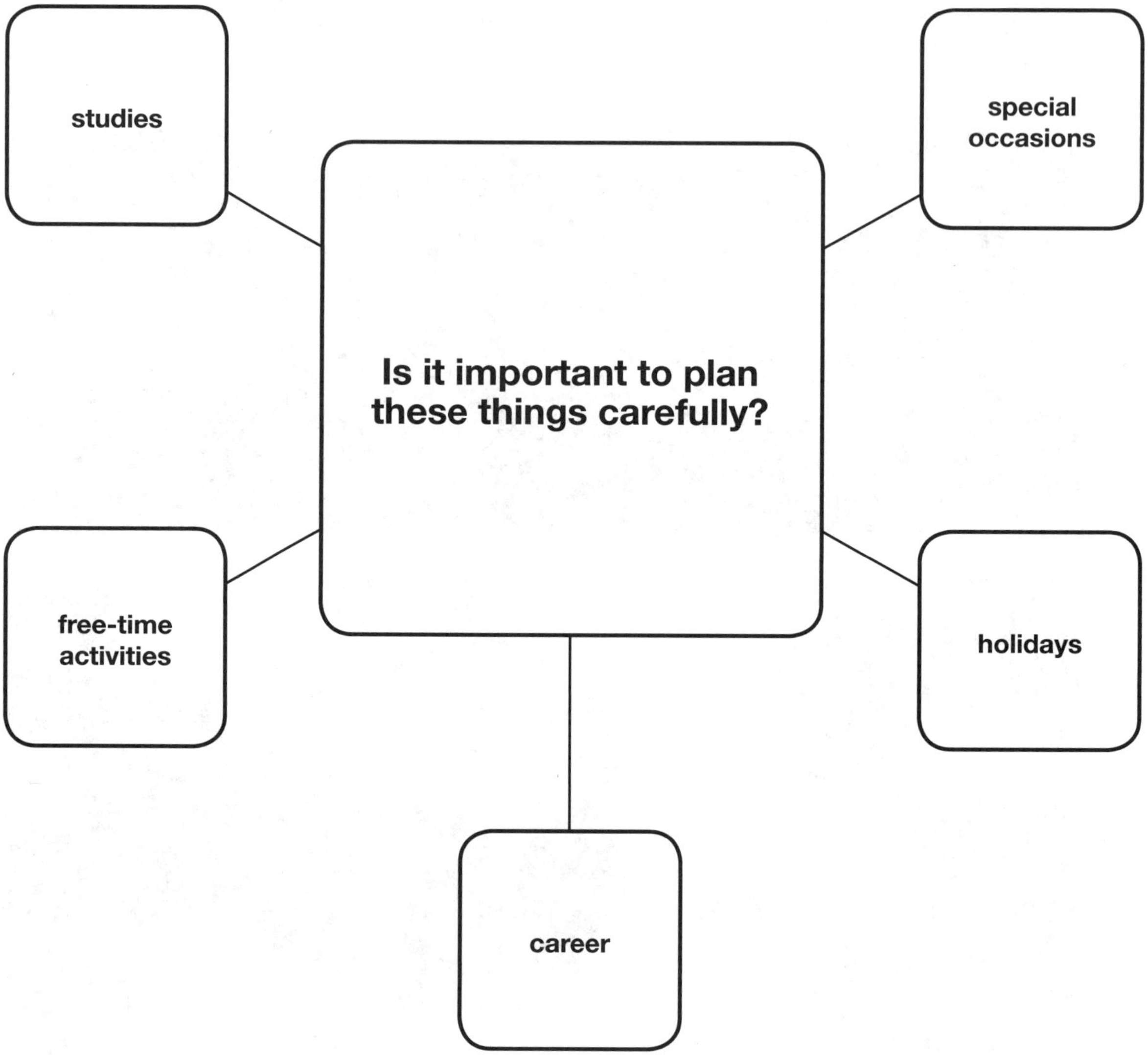
Is it important to plan these things carefully?
studies
special occasions
free-time activities
holidays
career

What are the people enjoying about spending time in the forest?

2A

2B

Why do the people need help in these situations?

2C

2D

2E

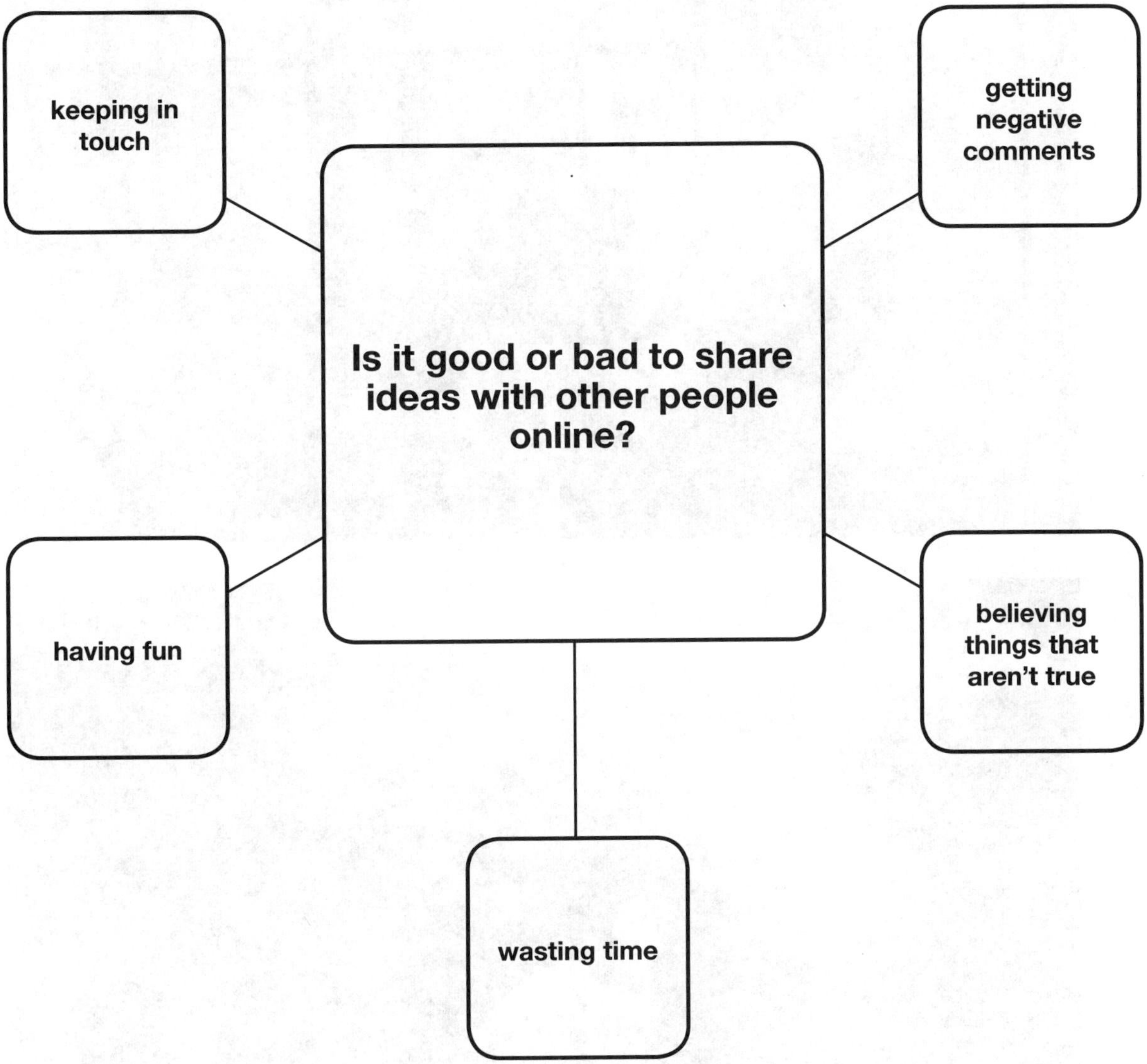
Is it good or bad to share ideas with other people online?
keeping in touch
getting negative comments
having fun
believing things that aren't true
wasting time

Why are the people resting in these places?

3A

3B

What are the people enjoying about their music?

3C

3D

3E

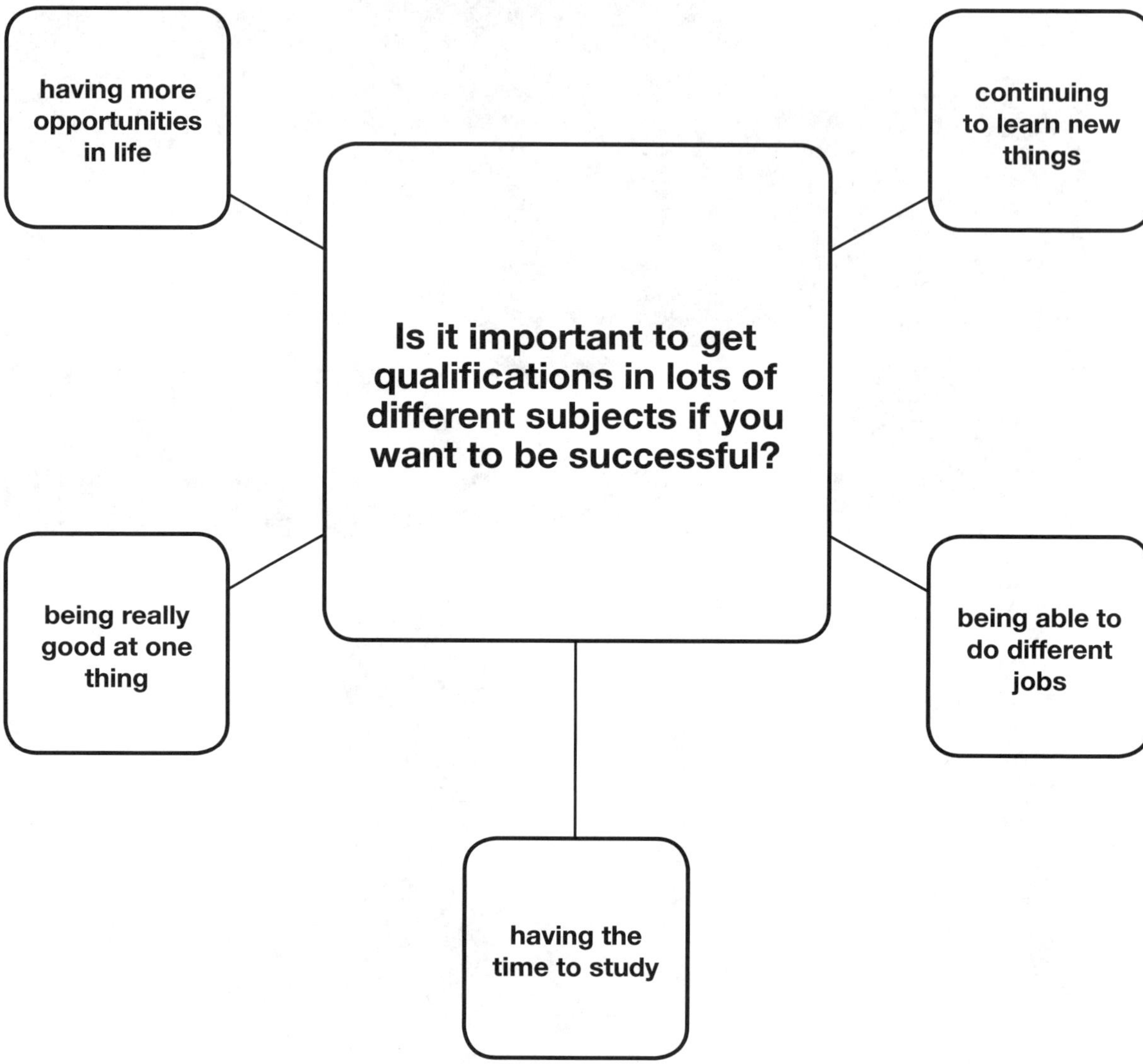
Is it important to get qualifications in lots of different subjects if you want to be successful?
having more opportunities in life
continuing to learn new things
being really good at one thing
being able to do different jobs
having the time to study

Why are the people preparing food in these situations?

4A

4B

Why are the people writing in these situations?

4C

4D

4E

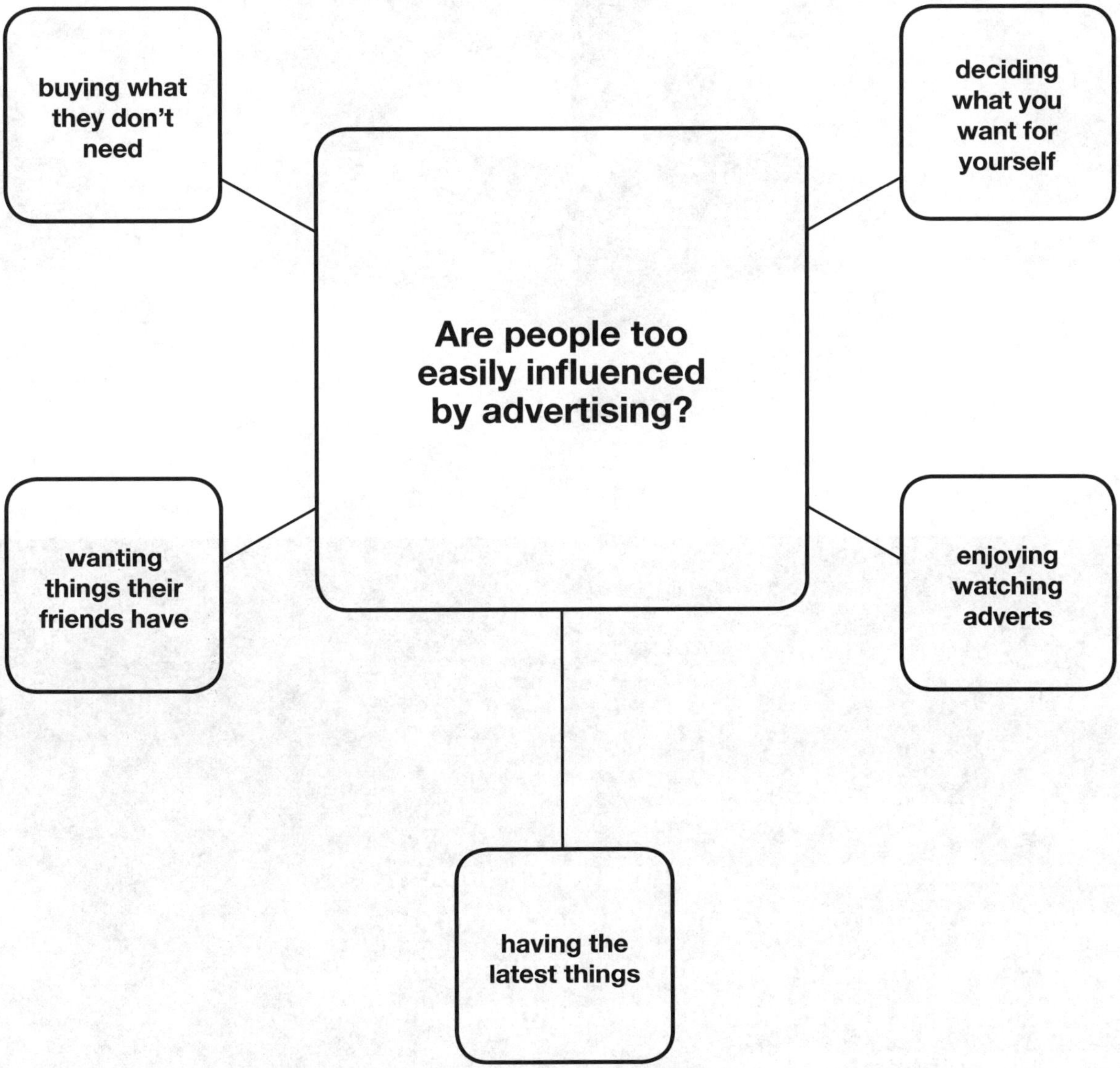
Are people too easily influenced by advertising?
buying what they don't need
deciding what you want for yourself
wanting things their friends have
enjoying watching adverts
having the latest things

Caiaimage/Sam Edwards/Getty In

SPOT THE DIFFERENCE

That's right – there is no difference.

All our authentic practice tests go through the same design process as the official exam. We check every single part of our practice tests with real students under exam conditions, to make sure we give you the most authentic experience possible.

The official practice tests from Cambridge.